Accounting for Restaurants and Bars

Steven M. Bragg

AccountingTools®

Published by AccountingTools, Inc., Centennial, Colorado.

ISBN 978-1-64221-134-4

For more information about AccountingTools® products, visit our Web site at www.accountingtools.com.

Table of Contents

About the Author

Steven Bragg, CPA, has been the chief financial officer or controller of four companies, as well as a consulting manager at Ernst & Young. He received a master's degree in finance from Bentley College, an MBA from Babson College, and a Bachelor's degree in Economics from the University of Maine. He has been a two-time president of the Colorado Mountain Club, and is an avid alpine skier, mountain biker, and certified master diver. Mr. Bragg resides in Centennial, Colorado. He has written more than 300 books and courses, including *New Controller Guidebook, GAAP Guidebook,* and *Payroll Management.*

Steven maintains the accountingtools.com web site, which contains continuing professional education courses, the Accounting Best Practices podcast, and thousands of articles on accounting subjects.

Accounting for Restaurants and Bars

Introduction

Accounting involves the recordation of business transactions, which are then aggregated into financial reports. This is an especially critical function in the restaurant and bar business, where margins are thin, and managers need to have a deep understanding of operations in order to generate a profit. In this book, we cover all aspects of the accounting transactions, reports, and metrics of restaurants and bars, along with several related topics.

Characteristics of Restaurants and Bars

Restaurants and bars have several unique characteristics that impact the structure and type of accounting systems used. These characteristics are as follows:

- *Inventory spoilage.* The food inventory of a restaurant spoils very quickly. In order to avoid losses on spoiled food, a restaurant has to maintain tight control over the amount of inventory on hand, and only replenish enough to meet its immediate needs.
- *Nature of employees.* The employees of restaurants and bars are usually paid low wages, which leads to continual turnover. In this environment, it is easy to hire someone without a strong sense of ethics, who is willing to steal from the business. This calls for strong controls to offset the actions of employees.
- *Profit margins.* Most restaurants operate on very slim profit margins, due to intense competition from other restaurants. Even modest cost increases in a few areas could trigger a loss, so restaurant owners need unusually detailed and frequent financial reports to tell them when something is wrong.
- *Separation of duties.* There are not enough people working in most restaurants to have a proper separation of duties, which increases the risk of employee theft. This is a particular concern in a bar operation, where the bartender not only takes customer orders, but also fulfills them and accepts payment.
- *Theft risk.* The nature of a restaurant or bar makes it more subject to theft. For example, if one of these businesses accepts large amounts of cash, then employees may skim it, or a variety of stratagems can be employed to steal it after the fact. In addition, it is easy to consume inventory (food or drinks) on the premises, or walk out with it.
- *Transaction volume.* Restaurants process large numbers of transactions every day, and usually concentrated within a few hours. This concentration and volume make it difficult to oversee each one in detail to ensure that it has been processed correctly.

The Uniform System of Accounts

The *chart of accounts* is a listing of all accounts used in an organization's general ledger. It is used by the accounting software to aggregate information into the entity's financial statements. The chart is usually sorted in order by account number, to ease the task of locating specific accounts. The accounts are usually numeric, but can also be alphabetic or alphanumeric.

Accounts are usually listed in order of their appearance in the financial statements, starting with the balance sheet and continuing with the income statement. Thus, the chart of accounts begins with cash, proceeds through liabilities and shareholders' equity, and then continues with accounts for revenues and then expenses.

What should be the layout of this chart of accounts? The National Restaurant Association (NRA) has developed a *Uniform System of Accounts for Restaurants*, which lays out a detailed set of accounts that can be used, along with the associated identifying account numbers. The intent behind using this chart of accounts is that the NRA has done a thorough job of including every possible account that might be of interest to a business owner, so that every possible transaction can be separately recorded. It is also useful to follow this format, so that the results of several restaurants can be reliably compared to each other – as long as each restaurant in a comparison group stores transactions in the same manner, using the same accounts. While this chart of accounts will certainly cover your needs, a smaller restaurant with more limited offerings could likely skip a number of the accounts.

We have provided a sample restaurant chart of accounts in the following two exhibits, which start account numbering at 1000 and allocate accounts to different clusters of assets, liabilities, and so forth in blocks of 100. We set intervals between account numbers in order to provide space for additional accounts to be entered at a later date, as the need arises.

Sample Restaurant Chart of Accounts (Balance Sheet Accounts)

Account Number	Account Name	Account Number	Account Name
1000	CASH (asset)	2000	PAYABLES (liability)
1005	Cash on hand	2005	Trade payables
1010	Operating bank account	2010	Other payables
1015	Savings bank account	2100	PAYROLL TAXES PAYABLE (liability)
1100	RECEIVABLES (asset)	2105	Withholding and FICA taxes
1105	Trade receivables	2110	Unemployment taxes
1110	Employee advances	2200	SALES TAXES PAYABLE (liability)
1115	Allowance for doubtful accounts	2205	Sales taxes payable
1200	INVENTORY (asset)	2210	Liquor taxes payable
1205	Food inventory	2300	ACCRUED EXPENSES (liability)
1210	Soft drinks inventory	2305	Employee compensation
1215	Liquor inventory	2310	Accrued vacation
1220	Beer inventory	2315	Accrued rent
1225	Wine inventory	2320	Accrued real estate taxes
1230	Merchandise inventory	2325	Accrued personal property taxes
1235	Supplies inventory	2330	Other accrued liabilities
1300	PREPAID EXPENSES (asset)	2400	OTHER LIABILITIES (liability)
1305	Prepaid insurance	2405	Gift certificates
1310	Prepaid taxes	2410	Customer deposits
1315	Prepaid other	2415	Charge tips withheld
1400	FIXED ASSETS (asset)	2420	Other liabilities
1405	Building	2500	CURRENT PORTION OF DEBT (liability)
1410	Furniture and fixtures	2505	Current portion of notes payable
1415	Land	2600	LONG-TERM DEBT (liability)
1420	Leasehold improvements	2605	Notes payable
1425	Vehicles	2610	Less: Current portion of notes payable
1430	Accumulated depreciation	3000	EQUITY (equity)
1500	OTHER ASSETS (asset)	3005	Common stock
1505	Organizational costs	3010	Additional paid-in capital
1510	Pre-opening costs	3015	Retained earnings
1515	Liquor license		
1520	Other assets		

Sample Restaurant Chart of Accounts (Income Statement Accounts)

Account Number	Account Name	Account Number	Account Name
4000	SALES (revenue)	7015	Music licensing fees
4005	Food sales	7020	Television broadcast fees
4010	Soft drinks	7100	MARKETING (expense)
4015	Liquor	7105	Advertising
4020	Beer	7110	Direct response marketing
4025	Wine	7115	Discounts and coupons
4030	Merchandise	7120	Public relations
4035	Vending machines	7125	Research activities
4100	OTHER SALES (revenue)	7130	Reservation system
4105	Banquet room rental	7135	Website maintenance
4110	Cover charges	7200	COMPENSATION (expense)
4115	Delivery charges	7205	Management compensation
4120	Vending commissions	7210	Staff compensation – back of house
4125	Valet parking	7215	Staff compensation – front of house
5000	COST OF SALES (expense)	7220	Staff compensation – administration
5005	Food cost	7300	EMPLOYEE BENEFITS (expense)
5010	Soft drink cost	7305	Payroll taxes
5015	Liquor cost	7310	Medical insurance
5020	Beer cost	7315	Disability insurance
5025	Wine cost	7320	Life insurance
5030	Merchandise cost	7325	Pension plan expenses
5035	Paper cost	7330	Workers' compensation insurance
6000	Direct Operating Expenses (expense)	7335	Employee meals
6005	China and glassware	7340	Employee activities
6010	Cleaning supplies	7400	UTILITIES (expense)
6015	Flowers and decorations	7405	Electricity
6020	Kitchen fuel	7410	Gas
6025	Kitchen utensils	7415	Trash removal
6030	Laundry and linen	7420	Water and sewage
6035	Licenses	7500	ADMINISTRATIVE (expense)
6040	Menus and wine lists	7505	Bad debts
6045	Paper supplies	7510	Bank / Credit card fees
6050	Silverware	7515	Depreciation
6055	Uniforms	7520	Licenses and permits
7000	ENTERTAINMENT (expense)	7525	Professional services
7005	Musicians and entertainers	7530	Rent
7010	Meals served to performers	7535	Real estate taxes
		7540	Interest expense
		7545	Income taxes

Some of the accounts noted in the preceding chart of accounts are unique to the restaurant and bar industry, or at least relate to transactions that are more commonly found within that industry. In the following bullet points, we describe some of these accounts:

- *Cash on hand (asset).* Many businesses do not maintain any cash on the premises, but this is not the case in the restaurant and bar industry, where some customers prefer to pay with cash. Consequently, a certain amount of cash is maintained on the premises to handle these transactions.

- *Accounts receivable (asset).* Restaurants mostly deal with payments at the point of sale, but there are cases in which customers will be billed for meals provided – usually in relation to larger parties where the accountant must tally up the amount of food and drinks provided, and then bills the customer for this amount. Some customers may also be provided with house accounts, where they can run up a bill over several visits and are then invoiced at regular intervals.

- *Inventory (asset).* Inventories vary substantially from those of other businesses. A restaurant or bar should maintain separate accounts for each type of inventory, with separate accounts for food, liquor, beer, wine, and merchandise. It may also be useful to maintain an inventory account for paper products.

- *China, glassware, silver, and linen (fixed asset).* Most fixed asset accounts are similar to those found in other businesses, but a separate account can be useful for tracking the cost of china, glassware, silver, and linen. Some accountants prefer to charge these purchases to expense as incurred, especially when the amounts involved are minor.

- *Leasehold improvements (fixed asset).* Restaurant and bar owners commonly lease the premises from which they provide services, so any significant additions to these spaces are recorded as leasehold improvements. This asset is amortized over the lesser of its useful life or the life of the lease, after which the landlord takes possession.

- *Liquor license (other assets).* When it is necessary to purchase a liquor license, the amount paid can be recorded as an asset.

- *Deposits on banquets (liability).* This account is needed when customers pay in advance for a banquet. This is initially recorded as a liability, which is converted into a sale once the banquet takes place.

- *Gift certificates outstanding (liability).* A restaurant or bar may sell gift cards, in which case they are initially recorded as a liability until they are cashed in by the gift card recipient; at that point, they are recorded as a sale. Depending on the applicable state law, unredeemed gift cards may be classified as unclaimed property, in which case they are remitted to the state government.

- *Utilities.* The cost of utilities is especially important for a restaurant, since it uses significantly more energy than other types of businesses. This is because of the energy-intensive cooking and washing operations, as well as the high-output HVAC systems needed to maintain pleasant temperatures in the dining area.

Restaurant and Bar Financial Statements

Restaurants and bars normally issue a set of financial statements that are formatted in the same manner from period to period, in order to enhance their comparability over time. The income statement records revenues and expenses for the reporting period, while the balance sheet reveals the ending asset, liability and equity account balances for that period. The statement of cash flows shows the cash inflows and outflows of the business, broken down into several categories.

The Income Statement

One of the best revenue and cost control mechanisms for a business is the income statement, which summarizes the revenues, expenses, and profit or loss of a restaurant or bar for a designated period of time. An essential element of this layout is that food and alcoholic beverage sales be reported separately, since many state governments require that beverage sales be reported to them. A sample income statement in a summarized format appears in the following exhibit.

Income Statement
For the Month Ended March 31, 20X1

Sales:		
Food	$800,000	80%
Beverage	200,000	20%
Total Sales	$1,000,000	100%
Cost of Sales:		
Food	280,000	35%
Beverage	40,000	20%
Total Cost of Sales	320,000	32%
Gross Profit:		
Food	520,000	65%
Beverage	160,000	80%
Total Gross Profit	680,000	68%
Operating Expenses:		
Compensation	250,000	25%
Employee benefits	30,000	3%
Direct operating expenses	80,000	8%
Marketing	30,000	3%
Utilities	40,000	4%
Repairs and maintenance	30,000	3%
Administrative	50,000	5%
Occupancy	90,000	9%
Depreciation	20,000	2%
Total Operating Expenses	620,000	62%
Operating Income	60,000	6%
Interest	30,000	3%
Income taxes	10,000	1%
Net income	$20,000	2%

An essential component of this income statement is the percentage column on the far right side, which shows each expense as a percentage of revenues. This is a useful tracking mechanism for identifying which costs appear to be trending higher as a percentage of revenue, and is a good starting point for a more detailed analysis of costs incurred. Another good control mechanism in the report is the separate reporting of a gross profit for food sales and beverage sales. These two revenue classifications have very different gross profits, so it makes sense to report them separately, and track them over time to detect any significant changes.

A key item in the preceding income statement was a summary-level line item called *direct operating expenses*. This line item is the aggregation of a number of smaller expenses related to the running of a restaurant, and typically contains the following items:

- China and glassware
- Cleaning supplies
- Flowers and decorations
- Kitchen fuel
- Kitchen utensils
- Laundry and linen
- Licenses
- Menus and wine lists
- Paper supplies
- Silverware
- Uniforms

For analysis purposes, it can be useful to create a secondary report that itemizes each of the expenses that sum up to the direct operating expenses line item in the income statement.

Profit Centers

A *profit center* is a business unit within a restaurant that generates revenues and profits or losses. A restaurant may have a number of profit centers, such as for banquets, bar, and food service. It is highly advisable for the restaurant owner to create and track separate income statements for each of these profit centers, in order to investigate any anomalies in the reported revenues and expenses, as well as to better understand where profits (and losses) are being generated.

Similar Unit Comparisons

It can be useful to structure an income statement in the format shown in the preceding exhibit, but with the results of additional operating units also listed. This is a useful format when you own a number of similar restaurants or bars, and want to compare their results. While anomalies between the locations might be due to simple differences in foot traffic and customer preferences by location, it is also possible that some units are better run than others, and so are able to achieve better results. If so, a similar unit comparison can spotlight which revenue or expense line items are the beneficiaries of this management performance, which can lead to best practices being adopted across all of the units.

The Balance Sheet

The balance sheet presents a firm's assets, liabilities, and equity as of the date of the report. This information is quite useful for lenders, who want to compare the amount of money invested in the enterprise to its outstanding debt (the debt-equity ratio) to decide whether it is excessively leveraged. Leverage is the use of debt to finance an entity's activities and asset purchases. When debt is the primary form of financing, a business is considered to be highly leveraged. The balance sheet can also be used to examine whether a restaurant or bar has enough cash on hand to pay for its short-term obligations.

A sample balance sheet in a summary format appears in the following statement.

Balance Sheet
As of 12/31/20X3

ASSETS	
Current Assets	
Cash	$80,000
Accounts receivable (net)	20,000
Inventories:	
Food	15,000
Beverage	10,000
Other	2,000
Prepaid expenses	5,000
Long-Term Assets	
Fixed assets (net)	500,000
Other assets	30,000
TOTAL ASSETS	$662,000
LIABILITIES	
Current Liabilities	
Accounts payable	$60,000
Other payables	10,000
Accrued expenses	12,000
Current portion of debt	20,000
Long-Term Liabilities	
Notes payable (net)	200,000
TOTAL LIABILITIES	302,000
SHAREHOLDERS' EQUITY	
Capital stock	160,000
Retained earnings	200,000
Total Equity	360,000
TOTAL LIABILITIES AND SHAREHOLDERS' EQUITY	$662,000

In the preceding balance sheet, a number of the line items are aggregated, containing all of the accounts shown in the previous chart of accounts pertaining to the balance sheet. This is done in order to make the balance sheet more readable, rather than presenting an excessively lengthy document that could potentially be several pages long. In particular, note that the accounts receivable, fixed assets, and notes payable line items are listed "net". This means that the accounts receivable are reduced by the allowance for doubtful accounts, while the fixed assets are reduced by accumulated depreciation, and the notes payables are reduced by that portion already presented as being payable in the current period. Thus, the "net" concept means that the various accounts aggregated into a line item contain at least one account that reduces the total presented amount.

The Statement of Cash Flows

The final financial statement used by a restaurant or bar is the statement of cash flows. This report shows the sources and uses of funds from a firm's operating, investing, and financing activities for the period covered by the report. A source of cash is one that provides cash to a restaurant or bar, while a use of cash is one that requires a cash outflow. For example, food inventory, beverage inventory, and expenditures for leasehold improvements all represent uses of cash, because you must pay cash in order to acquire them. Conversely, liabilities are a source of cash, because you are obtaining cash in exchange for a future payment back to the creditor or lender. For example, if a restaurant takes out a $50,000 loan, this represents a source of cash. In the following exhibit, we note the impact on cash flows of a variety of common situations that a restaurant or bar is likely to experience.

Sources and Uses of Cash

Event	Impact on Cash Flows
Pay suppliers by issuing them checks	This is a use of cash, since the amount in the checking account declines.
Collect outstanding receivables	This is a source of cash, since a receivable is being converted into cash.
Purchase food inventory	This is a use of cash, since a supplier is being paid for the inventory.
Increase a prepaid expense	When you make a payment that is then recorded as a prepaid expense (which is a current asset), this represents a use of cash.
Buy a marketable security	A purchase of a marketable security is a use of cash, since it results in a decline in your cash balance.
Sell restaurant equipment	The sale of restaurant equipment (or any other asset) is a source of cash, since a fixed asset is being converted into cash.
Increase accumulated depreciation	The recordation of depreciation expense increases the accumulated depreciation contra-asset account. This lowers the taxable income

Event	Impact on Cash Flows
	of the restaurant, and therefore the amount of income taxes to be paid. Consequently, this is a source of funds.
Record a supplier invoice	Whenever you record a supplier invoice, this indicates that the restaurant has benefited from goods or services being delivered to it without any offsetting cash payout (yet). Therefore, this is a source of funds.
Pay a supplier invoice	When you pay for an existing supplier invoice, this represents a use of cash, since the balance in the checking account is drawn down in order to pay for it.
Take on a loan	Whenever you take on a loan, you are accepting cash from a lender in exchange for a longer-term obligation to pay it back. Therefore, this is a source of cash.
Increase in accrued expenses	An increase in any type of accrued expense represents a source of funds, since you are receiving goods or services without an immediate obligation to pay for them.
Sale of common stock	Whenever you sell shares to investors, this results in a direct infusion of cash into the business, and is therefore a source of cash.

Tip: In short, any increase in assets represents a use of funds, while any decrease in assets is a source of funds. Conversely, any increase in liabilities represents a source of funds, while any decrease in liabilities represents a use of funds.

The statement of cash flows can be used to discern trends in restaurant or bar performance that are not readily apparent in the rest of the financial statements. It is especially useful when there is a divergence between the amount of profits reported and the amount of net cash flow generated by operations. Many investors feel that the statement of cash flows is the most transparent of the financial statements (i.e., most difficult to fudge), and so they tend to rely on it more than the other financial statements to discern the true performance of a restaurant.

There can be significant differences between the results shown in the income statement and the cash flows in this statement, for the following reasons:

- There are timing differences between the recordation of a transaction and when the related cash is actually expended or received.
- Management may be using aggressive revenue recognition to report revenue for which cash receipts are still some time in the future.
- The business may be asset intensive, and so requires large capital investments that do not appear in the income statement, except on a delayed basis as depreciation.

Cash flows in the statement are divided into the following three areas:

- *Cash flows from operating activities*. These constitute the revenue-generating activities of the restaurant. Examples of operating activities are cash received and disbursed for food and beverage purchases and sales, and payroll. Interest and taxes paid would also be included in this category. Cash inflows would be caused by the sale of food and beverages, as well as from any interest or dividend income on investments. Cash outflows would be caused by the purchase of food and beverage inventory, as well as from compensation payments to employees, payroll taxes, rent payments, and utilities.
- *Cash flows from investing activities*. These constitute payments made to acquire long-term assets, as well as cash received from their sale. Examples of investing activities are the purchase of fixed assets and the purchase or sale of securities issued by other entities, both of which would be cash outflows. Conversely, cash inflows would come from the sale of assets and the sale of investments.
- *Cash flows from financing activities*. These constitute activities that will alter the equity or borrowings of a restaurant. Examples are the sale of company shares, and the repurchase of shares and dividend payments. The sale of shares would be a source of cash, while the repurchase of shares and the issuance of dividends to investors would be uses of cash.

A good way to analyze a statement of cash flows is to compare it to the same report from the preceding year. Assuming that a firm's capacity has not changed in the interim, the two reports should yield fairly similar outcomes. You can then focus on any differences that have arisen in the most recent report.

A sample statement of cash flows follows.

Statement of Cash Flow
For the year ended 12/31/20X1

Net Cash Flow from Operating Activities		
Net income		$85,000
Reconciling items:		
Depreciation	$40,000	
Decrease in accounts receivable	12,000	
Increase in inventory	-4,000	
Increase in accounts payable	1,000	
Increase in accrued payroll	2,000	
Net cash flow from operating activities		136,000
Investing Activities		
Sale of investments	8,000	
Purchase of investments	-23,000	
Purchase of assets	-31,000	
Net cash flow from investing activities		-46,000
Financing Activities		
Payment of debt	-32,000	
Dividends paid to shareholders	-18,000	
Net cash flow from financing activities		-$50,000
Net increase in cash in 20X1		$125,000
Cash at beginning of 20X1		30,000
Cash at end of 20X1		$155,000

Inventory Accounting

In the next few sections, we cover the accounting for selected assets and liabilities of a restaurant or bar. In this section, we cover inventory tracking systems, inventory valuation methods, inventory spoilage, and several related issues.

Inventory Tracking Systems

A restaurant or bar manager should track the amount of inventory on hand at all times, in order to know when to place reorders. The simplest system for doing so is the physical inventory system, where a complete count of the inventory is conducted at regular intervals. A sample inventory count sheet (quite abbreviated) appears in the following exhibit.

16

Sample Inventory Count Sheet

Item Description	Unit Size	Par Level	Quantity on Hand	Cost	Extended Cost
Filet mignon	20 lb. case	6	6	$200.00	$1,200.00
Pork chops	lb.	30	20	10.50	210.00
Eggs	dz.	25	10	2.50	25.00
Sour cream	gal	3	1	12.00	12.00
Bread	loaf	25	15	2.25	33.75
Rolls	dz.	35	23	5.20	119.60

The *par level* stated in the preceding inventory count sheet is short for periodic automatic replacement, and represents the minimum amount of inventory needed to meet the demands of your customers, while providing a cushion in case of any unexpected demand. When the actual inventory level drops below the par level, it is time to place a restocking order. In the preceding exhibit, quite a few of the listed items have dropped below their par level, so reorders should be implemented at once.

Counting the inventory at regular intervals can be a simple matter for a smaller restaurant, but can be a significant waste of time when there is a large amount of inventory on hand. In the latter case, a perpetual inventory system may be a better choice. Under a perpetual inventory system, the inventory records are constantly updated for receipts and withdrawals. Perpetual systems are especially common for tracking inventories of alcoholic beverages, where a hand-held bar code scanner can be used to rapidly enter receipts and withdrawals. The main concern with the perpetual inventory system is the risk that key transactions may not be entered into the system at all, resulting in an incorrect on-hand balance.

Unit of Measure Issues

A *unit of measure* is the standard unit of measurement used when accounting for stock. This is a particular problem in the restaurant business, because so many different units of measure are used. For example, a unit of measure may be a case of cans, or it may be a gallon of milk, a quart of sour cream, or a case of apples. When counting inventory, it is essential to count in the correct unit of measure, or else the inventory valuation will be seriously inaccurate. For example, if you count a case of 12 cans (for which the purchase price was $30 for the entire case) and record each can as a separate item, then you will end up with an inventory valuation of $360 when it should be just $30.

Beverage Inventory Counts

Counting ending inventory for beverages can be difficult, because the amount of beverages in open containers can be difficult to ascertain. Here are three possible ways to count beverage quantities:

- *Count by fraction full.* This involves assigning a fraction to each bottle, based on how full it appears to be. For example, you could judge a bottle to be 10%,

20%, or 30% full. While this approach only approximates the true contents of a bottle, many accountants would consider it to be close enough.

- *Count by ruler*. A more accurate approach than counting by tenths of a bottle (in the preceding item) is to measure the fill height of each bottle with a ruler. This approach is a bit slower than counting by the fraction full.
- *Count by weight*. This involves weighing each open bottle, and then subtracting the weight of the empty bottle.

First In First Out Inventory Valuation

Given the serious obsolescence issues with food inventory, most restaurants prefer to use the *first in, first out* (FIFO) method for valuing their inventory. This accounting concept quite reasonably assumes that the first units received are the first ones used – which is a necessity when food items may spoil in just a few days. Under the FIFO approach, ending inventory is valued at the price most recently paid for it. For example, a restaurant has three cases of canned vegetables in stock at the end of the month. Its purchase history for these items is as follows:

- $25 for a case purchased on March 10
- $24 for two cases purchased on March 17
- $23 for a case purchased on March 25
- $22 for a case purchased on March 30

Under the FIFO approach, the three cases would be valued by working backwards in time. One case would be valued at $22, the next case at $23, and the final case at $24, for a total inventory valuation of $69. The earlier purchases would be ignored, since the associated cases are no longer in stock.

Inventory Spoilage

A major concern for any restaurant manager is inventory spoilage. Many food items have extremely short shelf lives, and so must be thrown out once those dates have passed. This means that spoilage is likely the single largest inventory issue faced by a restaurant. From an accounting perspective, it is not an especially difficult issue to ascertain – just review the food receipt date or sell-by date, or conduct a visual review for clearly spoiled products, and write down the inventory at the end of each month by the amount of the food items thrown out.

Delivery Problems

There may be times when a food supplier does not provide the full amount of what you ordered, as can be discovered through a detailed receiving inspection. This inspection may also result in the refusal of certain food items, perhaps because they have been damaged or have gone bad. When this is the case, you should fill out a credit memo, which notes the items not delivered, or which have been rejected. A copy of this document is then sent to the supplier, who is expected to process a credit against the applicable invoice. A sample credit memo appears in the following exhibit.

Sample Credit Memo

CREDIT MEMO					
Supplier:			**Delivery Date:**		
Invoice #:			**Credit Memo #:**		
Correction					
Item	Quantity	Short	Rejected	Price	Credit
Total					
Original invoice $:		**Less: Credit Memo $:**		**Adjusted Invoice Total:**	
Additional information:					
Supplier representative:					
Restaurant representative:					

Accounting for Fixed Assets

A restaurant will need to invest in a substantial amount of fixed assets, including land, buildings, leasehold improvements, furniture and fixtures, and computer software. Given the importance of this asset class, we provide an expanded treatment of the accounting for fixed assets in this section, including the range of possible classifications, depreciation concepts, asset disposals, and the related accounting entries.

Fixed Asset Classifications

If an expenditure qualifies as a fixed asset, it must be recorded within an account classification. Account classifications are used to aggregate fixed assets into groups, so that the same depreciation methods and useful lives can be applied to them.

You can create general ledger accounts by classification, and store fixed asset transactions within the classifications to which they belong. Here are the most common classifications used:

- *Buildings*. This account may include the cost of acquiring a building, or the cost of constructing one. If the purchase price of a building includes the cost of land, apportion some of the cost to the Land account (which is not depreciated).
- *Computer equipment*. This classification typically includes desktop and laptop computers, as well as pager reservation systems, though a restaurant might also invest in routers and servers. It is useful to set the capitalization limit[1] higher than the cost of minor computer equipment, so that an excessive number of these assets are not tracked.
- *Equipment*. This category includes all types of restaurant equipment, including beverage equipment, drive-through equipment, and kitchen equipment.
- *Furniture and fixtures*. This is one of the broadest categories of fixed assets, since it can include such diverse assets as dining room tables and chairs, restaurant accessories, and bar stools.
- *Intangible assets*. This is a non-physical asset, examples of which are trademarks and customer lists.
- *Land*. This is the only asset that is not depreciated, because it is considered to have an indeterminate useful life. Include in this category all expenditures to prepare the land for its intended purpose, such as demolishing an existing building or grading the land.
- *Land improvements*. Include any expenditures that add functionality to a parcel of land, such as irrigation systems, fencing, and landscaping.
- *Leasehold improvements*. These are improvements to leased space that are made by the tenant, and typically include the dining area, air conditioning, telephone wiring, and related permanent fixtures.
- *Office equipment*. This account contains such equipment as copiers and printers.
- *Software*. Includes the point of sale (POS) software[2], timekeeping, bar control system, and back office software used by a restaurant or bar, though these packages might be rented instead.
- *Vehicles*. This account contains automobiles, delivery trucks, and similar types of rolling stock.

---

[1] The capitalization limit is the amount paid for an asset, above which it is recorded as a long-term asset. If the amount paid is less than the capitalization limit, then the amount paid is instead charged to expense in the period incurred.

[2] A point of sale system can contain a number of features specific to a restaurant or bar, such as recording sales, accumulating sales information by server, transmitting orders to the kitchen, compiling guest checks, credit card processing, time tracking, and identifying such special transactions as discounted meals, complimentary meals, employee meals, and voids. Those POS systems loaded with the most comprehensive features can be quite expensive.

Initial Measurement of a Fixed Asset

Initially record a fixed asset at the historical cost of acquiring it, which includes the costs to bring it to the condition and location necessary for its intended use. If these preparatory activities will occupy a period of time, also include in the cost of the asset the interest costs related to the cost of the asset during the preparation period. The inclusion of interest costs provides a truer picture of the total investment in an asset.

The activities involved in bringing a fixed asset to the condition and location necessary for its intended purpose include the following:

- Physical construction of the asset
- Demolition of any preexisting structures
- Renovating a preexisting structure to alter it for use by the buyer
- Administrative and technical activities during preconstruction for such activities as designing the asset and obtaining permits
- Administrative and technical work after construction commences for such activities as litigation, labor disputes, and technical problems

Depreciation Concepts

The purpose of *depreciation* is to charge to expense a portion of an asset that relates to the revenue generated by that asset. This is called the matching principle, where revenues and expenses both appear in the income statement in the same reporting period, which gives the best view of how well a restaurant has performed in a given accounting period. The trouble with this matching concept is that there is usually only a tenuous connection between the generation of revenue and a specific asset.

To get around this linkage problem, we usually assume a steady rate of depreciation over the useful life of each asset, so that we approximate a linkage between the recognition of revenues and expenses. This approximation threatens our credulity even more when a business uses accelerated depreciation, since the main reason for using it is to defer taxes (and not to better match revenues and expenses).

If we were not to use depreciation at all, we would be forced to charge all assets to expense as soon as we buy them. This would result in large losses in the months when the purchase transaction occurs, followed by unusually high profitability in those periods when the corresponding amount of revenue is recognized, with no offsetting expense. Thus, a restaurant or bar that does not use depreciation will have front-loaded expenses, and extremely variable financial results.

There are three factors to consider in the calculation of depreciation, which are as follows:

- *Useful life*. This is the time period over which it is expected that an asset will be productive. Past an asset's useful life, it is no longer cost-effective to continue operating the asset, so a business would dispose of it or stop using it. Depreciation is recognized over the useful life of an asset.
- *Salvage value*. When a business eventually disposes of an asset, it may be able to sell the asset for some reduced amount, which is the salvage value.

Depreciation is calculated based on the asset cost, less any estimated salvage value. If salvage value is expected to be quite small, it is generally ignored for the purpose of calculating depreciation.

EXAMPLE

The Masterson Family Restaurant buys a delivery van for $40,000 and estimates that its salvage value will be $10,000 in five years, when it plans to dispose of the van. This means that Masterson will depreciate $30,000 of the asset cost over five years, leaving $10,000 of the cost remaining at the end of that time. Masterson expects to then sell the van for $10,000, which will eliminate it from the firm's accounting records.

- *Depreciation method.* Depreciation expense can be calculated using an accelerated depreciation method, or evenly over the useful life of the asset. The advantage of using an accelerated method is that you can recognize more depreciation early in the life of a fixed asset, which defers some income tax expense recognition to a later period. The advantage of using a steady depreciation rate is the ease of calculation. An example of an accelerated depreciation method is the MACRS method (as described later). The primary method for steady depreciation is the straight-line method.

The Straight-Line Method

Under the straight-line method, you would depreciate an asset at the same standard rate throughout its useful life. To do so, recognize depreciation expense evenly over the estimated useful life of an asset. The straight-line calculation steps are:

1. Subtract the estimated salvage value of the asset from the amount at which it is recorded on the books.
2. Determine the estimated useful life of the asset. It is easiest to use a standard useful life for each class of assets.
3. Divide the estimated useful life (in years) into 1 to arrive at the straight-line depreciation rate.
4. Multiply the depreciation rate by the asset cost (less salvage value).

EXAMPLE

The Higgins Family Restaurant purchases a pizza oven for $6,000. It has an estimated salvage value of $1,000 and a useful life of five years. The accountant calculates the annual straight-line depreciation for the oven as follows:

1. Purchase cost of $6,000 – Estimated salvage value of $1,000 = Depreciable asset cost of $5,000
2. 1 ÷ 5-Year useful life = 20% Depreciation rate per year
3. 20% Depreciation rate × $5,000 Depreciable asset cost = $1,000 Annual depreciation

---

MACRS Depreciation

MACRS depreciation is the tax depreciation system used in the United States. MACRS is an acronym for Modified Accelerated Cost Recovery System. Under MACRS, fixed assets are assigned to a specific asset class. The Internal Revenue Service has published a complete set of depreciation tables for each of these classes. The classes are noted in the following table. Those assets that may be found in a restaurant have been stated in bold.

MACRS Table

Class	Depreciation Period	Description
3-year property	3 years	Tractor units for over-the-road use, race horses over 2 years old when placed in service, any other horse over 12 years old when placed in service, qualified rent-to-own property
5-year property	5 years	**Automobiles**, taxis, buses, **trucks, computers and peripheral equipment, office equipment**, any property used in research and experimentation, breeding cattle and dairy cattle, appliances and etc. used in residential rental real estate activity, certain green energy property
7-year property	7 years	**Office furniture and fixtures**, agricultural machinery and equipment, any property not designated as being in another class, natural gas gathering lines
10-year property	10 years	Vessels, barges, tugs, single-purpose agricultural or horticultural structures, trees/vines bearing fruits or nuts, qualified small electric meter and smart electric grid systems
15-year property	15 years	Certain **land improvements** (such as shrubbery, fences, roads, sidewalks and bridges), retail motor fuel outlets, municipal wastewater treatment plants, clearing and grading land improvements for gas utility property, electric transmission property, natural gas distribution lines
20-year property	20 years	Farm buildings (other than those noted under 10-year property), municipal sewers not categorized as 25-year

Class	Depreciation Period	Description
		property, the initial clearing and grading of land for electric utility transmission and distribution plants
25-year property	25 years	Property that is an integral part of the water distribution facilities, municipal sewers
Residential rental property	27.5 years	Any building or structure where 80% or more of its gross rental income is from dwelling units
Nonresidential real property	39 years	An office building, store, or warehouse that is not residential property or has a class life of less than 27.5 years

The depreciation rates associated with the more common asset classes are noted in the following exhibit.

Depreciation Rates for MACRS Asset Classes

Recovery Year	3-Year Property	5-Year Property	7-Year Property	10-Year Property	15-Year Property	20-Year Property
1	33.33%	20.00%	14.29%	10.00%	5.00%	3.750%
2	44.45%	32.00%	24.49%	18.00%	9.50%	7.219%
3	14.81%	19.20%	17.49%	14.40%	8.55%	6.677%
4	7.41%	11.52%	12.49%	11.52%	7.70%	6.177%
5		11.52%	8.93%	9.22%	6.93%	5.713%
6		5.76%	8.92%	7.37%	6.23%	5.285%
7			8.93%	6.55%	5.90%	4.888%
8			4.46%	6.55%	5.90%	4.522%
9				6.56%	5.91%	4.462%
10				6.55%	5.90%	4.461%
11				3.28%	5.91%	4.462%
12					5.90%	4.461%
13					5.91%	4.462%
14					5.90%	4.461%
15					5.91%	4.462%
16					2.95%	4.461%
17						4.462%
18						4.461%
19						4.462%
20						4.461%
21						2.231%

Depreciation is calculated for tax reporting purposes by aggregating assets into the various classes noted in the preceding exhibit and using the depreciation rates for each class. MACRS ignores salvage value.

The MACRS depreciation rates are used to determine the depreciation expense for taxable income, while other depreciation methods are used to arrive at the depreciation expense for net income. Since these depreciation methods have differing results, there will be a temporary difference between the book values of fixed assets under the two methods, which will gradually be resolved over their useful lives.

Accounting for Leasehold Improvements

Many restaurants and bars lease space from a third party, and then pay to build out the property with walls, air conditioning, telephone wiring, and related permanent fixtures. These improvements are known as leasehold improvements. In accounting, a leasehold improvement is considered an asset of the tenant if the tenant paid for it, the investment exceeds the capitalization limit of the tenant, and the improvements will be usable for more than one reporting period. If so, you (the tenant) record the investment as a fixed asset and amortize it over the lesser of the remaining term of the lease or the useful life of the improvements. Upon the termination of the lease, all leasehold improvements become the property of the landlord.

Depreciation Accounting Entries

The basic depreciation entry is to debit the depreciation expense account (which appears in the income statement) and credit the accumulated depreciation account (which appears in the balance sheet as an account that reduces the amount of fixed assets). Over time, the accumulated depreciation balance will continue to increase as more depreciation is added to it, until such time as it equals the original cost of the asset. At that time, stop recording any depreciation expense, since the cost of the asset has now been reduced to zero.

The journal entry for depreciation can be a simple two-line entry designed to accommodate all types of fixed assets, or it may be subdivided into separate entries for each type of fixed asset.

EXAMPLE

Pembroke Restaurants calculates that it should have $25,000 of depreciation expense in the current month. The entry is:

	Debit	Credit
Depreciation expense (expense)	25,000	
Accumulated depreciation (contra asset)		25,000

In the following month, Pembroke's accountant decides to show a higher level of precision at the expense account level, and instead elects to apportion the $25,000 of depreciation among different expense accounts, so that each class of asset has a separate depreciation charge. The entry is:

	Debit	Credit
Depreciation expense – automobiles (expense)	4,000	
Depreciation expense – kitchen equipment (expense)	10,000	
Depreciation expense – furniture and fixtures (expense)	6,000	
Depreciation expense – office equipment (expense)	3,000	
Depreciation expense – software (expense)	2,000	
Accumulated depreciation (contra asset)		25,000

The journal entry to record the amortization of intangible assets is fundamentally the same as the entry for depreciation, except that the accounts used substitute the word "amortization" for depreciation.

EXAMPLE

Pembroke Restaurants calculates that it should have $4,000 of amortization expense in the current month that is related to intangible assets. The entry is:

	Debit	Credit
Amortization expense (expense)	4,000	
Accumulated amortization (contra asset)		4,000

Accumulated Depreciation

When you sell or otherwise dispose of an asset, remove all related accumulated depreciation from the accounting records at the same time. Otherwise, an unusually large amount of accumulated depreciation will build up on the balance sheet.

EXAMPLE

Penn Central Eatery has $1,000,000 of fixed assets, for which it has charged $380,000 of accumulated depreciation. This results in the following presentation on Penn Central's balance sheet:

Fixed assets	$1,000,000
Less: Accumulated depreciation	(380,000)
Net fixed assets	$620,000

Penn Central then sells restaurant equipment for $80,000 that had an original cost of $140,000, and for which it had already recorded accumulated depreciation of $50,000. It records the sale with this journal entry:

	Debit	Credit
Cash – operating (asset)	80,000	
Accumulated depreciation (contra asset)	50,000	
Loss on asset sale (loss)	10,000	
Fixed assets (asset)		140,000

As a result of this entry, Penn Central's balance sheet presentation of fixed assets has changed, so that fixed assets before accumulated depreciation have declined to $860,000, and accumulated depreciation has declined to $330,000. The new balance sheet presentation is:

Fixed assets	$860,000
Less: Accumulated depreciation	(330,000)
Net fixed assets	$530,000

The amount of net fixed assets declined by $90,000 as a result of the asset sale, which is the sum of the $80,000 cash proceeds and the $10,000 loss resulting from the asset sale.

Asset Disposal Accounting

There are two scenarios under which you may dispose of a fixed asset. The first situation arises when a fixed asset is being eliminated without receiving any payment in return. This is a common situation when a fixed asset is being scrapped because it is obsolete or no longer in use, and there is no resale market for it. In this case, reverse any accumulated depreciation and reverse the original asset cost. If the asset is fully depreciated, that is the extent of the entry.

EXAMPLE

Bradbury Fast Food buys restaurant equipment for $10,000 and recognizes $1,000 of depreciation per year over the following ten years. At that time, the equipment is not only fully depreciated, but also ready for the scrap heap. Bradbury gives away the equipment for free, and records the following entry.

	Debit	Credit
Accumulated depreciation (contra asset)	10,000	
Fixed assets – equipment (asset)		10,000

A variation on this situation is to write off a fixed asset that has not yet been completely depreciated. In this case, write off the remaining undepreciated amount of the asset to a loss account.

EXAMPLE

To use the same example, Bradbury Fast Food gives away the equipment after eight years, when it has not yet depreciated $2,000 of the asset's original $10,000 cost. In this case, Bradbury records the following entry:

	Debit	Credit
Loss on asset disposal (loss)	2,000	
Accumulated depreciation (contra asset)	8,000	
Fixed assets – equipment (asset)		10,000

The second scenario arises when an asset is sold, so that the restaurant receives cash in exchange for the asset. Depending upon the price paid and the remaining amount of depreciation that has not yet been charged to expense, this can result in either a gain or a loss on sale of the asset.

EXAMPLE

Bradbury Fast Food still disposes of its $10,000 equipment, but does so after seven years, and sells it for $3,500 in cash. In this case, it has already recorded $7,000 of depreciation expense. The entry is:

	Debit	Credit
Cash – operating (asset)	3,500	
Accumulated depreciation (contra asset)	7,000	
Gain on asset disposal (gain)		500
Fixed assets – equipment (asset)		10,000

What if Bradbury had sold the equipment for $2,500 instead of $3,500? Then there would be a loss of $5,000 on the sale. The entry would be:

	Debit	Credit
Cash – operating (asset)	2,500	
Accumulated depreciation (contra asset)	7,000	
Loss on asset disposal (loss)	500	
Fixed assets – equipment (asset)		10,000

The "loss on asset disposal" or "gain on asset disposal" accounts noted in the preceding sample entries are called disposal accounts. They may be combined into a single account or used separately to store gains and losses resulting from the disposal of fixed assets.

Accounting for Leases

A restaurant or bar may enter into a variety of leasing arrangements, such as for equipment rentals, restaurant or bar space, and office space. A central concept of the accounting for leases is that the restaurant or bar (the lessee) should recognize the assets and liabilities that underlie each leasing arrangement. This concept results in the following recognition in the balance sheet of the lessee as of the lease commencement date:

- Recognize a liability to make lease payments to the lessor
- Recognize a right-of-use asset that represents the right of the lessee to use the leased asset during the lease term

There are a number of additional topics related to asset and liability recognition, which are covered in the following sub-sections.

Types of Leases

There are several types of lease designations, which differ if an entity is the lessee or the lessor. It is critical to determine the type of a lease, since the accounting varies by lease type. The choices for a **lessee** are that a lease can be designated as either a finance lease or an operating lease. In essence, a *finance lease* designation implies that the lessee has purchased the underlying asset (even though this may not actually be the case), while an *operating lease* designation implies that the lessee has obtained the use of the underlying asset for only a period of time. A lessee should classify a lease as a finance lease when <u>any</u> of the following criteria are met:

- *Ownership transfer*. Ownership of the underlying asset is shifted to the lessee by the end of the lease term.
- *Ownership option*. The lessee has a purchase option to buy the leased asset, and is reasonably certain to use it.
- *Lease term*. The lease term covers the major part of the underlying asset's remaining economic life. This is considered to be 75% or more of the remaining economic life of the underlying asset. This criterion is not valid if the lease commencement date is near the end of the asset's economic life, which is considered to be a date that falls within the last 25% of the underlying asset's total economic life.
- *Present value*. The present value of the sum of all lease payments and any lessee-guaranteed residual value matches or exceeds the fair value of the underlying asset. The present value is based on the interest rate implicit in the lease.

- *Specialization*. The asset is so specialized that it has no alternative use for the lessor following the lease term. In this situation, there are essentially no remaining benefits that revert to the lessor.

When none of the preceding criteria are met, the lessee must classify a lease as an operating lease.

Initial Measurement

As of the commencement date of a lease, the lessee measures the liability and the right-of-use asset associated with the lease. These measurements are derived as follows:

- *Lease liability*. This is the present value of the lease payments, discounted at the discount rate for the lease. This rate is the rate implicit in the lease when that rate is readily determinable. If not, the lessee instead uses its incremental borrowing rate.
- *Right-of-use asset*. This is the initial amount of the lease liability, plus any lease payments made to the lessor before the lease commencement date, plus any initial direct costs incurred, minus any lease incentives received.

EXAMPLE

Linger Wine Bar enters into a five-year lease, where the lease payments are $35,000 per year, payable at the end of each year. Linger incurs initial direct costs of $8,000. The rate implicit in the lease is 8%.

At the commencement of the lease, the lease liability is $139,745, which is calculated as $35,000 multiplied by the 3.9927 rate for the five-period present value of an ordinary annuity. The right-of-use asset is calculated as the lease liability plus the amount of the initial direct costs, for a total of $147,745.

Short-Term Leases

When a lease has a term of 12 months or less, the lessee can elect not to recognize lease-related assets and liabilities in the balance sheet. This election is made by class of asset. When a lessee makes this election, it should usually recognize the expense related to a lease on a straight-line basis over the term of the lease.

If the lease term changes so that the remaining term now extends more than 12 months beyond the end of the previously determined lease term or the lessee will likely purchase the underlying asset, the arrangement is no longer considered a short-term lease. In this situation, account for the lease as a longer-term lease as of the date when there was a change in circumstances.

Finance Leases

When a lessee has designated a lease as a finance lease, it should recognize the following over the term of the lease:

- The ongoing amortization of the right-of-use asset
- The ongoing amortization of the interest on the lease liability
- Any variable lease payments that are not included in the lease liability
- Any impairment of the right-of-use asset

The amortization period for the right-of-use asset is from the lease commencement date to the earlier of the end of the lease term or the end of the useful life of the asset. An exception is when it is reasonably certain that the lessee will exercise an option to purchase the asset, in which case the amortization period is through the end of the asset's useful life.

After the commencement date, the lessee increases the carrying amount of the lease liability to include the interest expense on the lease liability, while reducing the carrying amount by the amount of all lease payments made during the period. The interest on the lease liability is the amount that generates a constant periodic discount rate on the remaining liability balance.

After the commencement date, the lessee reduces the right-of-use asset by the amount of accumulated amortization and accumulated impairment (if any).

EXAMPLE

Scottish Eggs Restaurant agrees to a five-year lease of equipment that requires an annual $20,000 payment, due at the end of each year. At the end of the lease period, Scottish has the option to buy the equipment for $1,000. Since the expected residual value of the equipment at that time is expected to be $25,000, the large discount makes it reasonably certain that the purchase option will be exercised. At the commencement date of the lease, the fair value of the equipment is $120,000, with an economic life of eight years. The discount rate for the lease is 6%.

Scottish classifies the lease as a finance lease, since it is reasonably certain to exercise the purchase option.

The lease liability at the commencement date is $84,995, which is calculated as the present value of five payments of $20,000, plus the present value of the $1,000 purchase option payment, discounted at 6%. Scottish recognizes the right-of-use asset as the same amount, since there are no initial direct costs, lease incentives, or other types of payments made by Scottish, either at or before the commencement date.

Scottish amortizes the right-of-use asset over the eight-year expected useful life of the equipment, under the assumption that it will exercise the purchase option and therefore keep the equipment for the eight-year period.

As an example of the subsequent accounting for the lease, Scottish recognizes a first-year interest expense of $5,100 (calculated as 6% × $84,995 lease liability), and recognizes the amortization of the right-of-use asset in the amount of $10,624 (calculated as $84,995 ÷ 8 years). This results in a lease liability at the end of Year 1 that has been reduced to $70,095 (calculated as $84,995 + $5,100 interest - $20,000 lease payment) and a right-of-use asset that has been reduced to $74,371 (calculated as $84,995 - $10,624 amortization).

By the end of Year 5, which is when the lease terminates, the lease liability has been reduced to $1,000, which is the amount of the purchase option. Scottish exercises the option, which settles the remaining liability. At that time, the carrying amount of the right-of-use asset has declined to $31,875 (reflecting five years of amortization at $10,624 per year). Scottish shifts this amount into a fixed asset account, and depreciates it over the remaining three years of its useful life.

Operating Leases

When a lessee has designated a lease as an operating lease, the lessee should recognize the following over the term of the lease:

- A lease cost in each period, where the total cost of the lease is allocated over the lease term on a straight-line basis. This can be altered if there is another systematic and rational basis of allocation that more closely follows the benefit usage pattern to be derived from the underlying asset.
- Any variable lease payments that are not included in the lease liability
- Any impairment of the right-of-use asset

EXAMPLE

Epic Burgers enters into an operating lease in which the lease payment is $25,000 per year for the first five years and $30,000 per year for the next five years. These payments sum to $275,000 over ten years. Epic will therefore recognize a lease expense of $27,500 per year for all of the years in the lease term.

At any point in the life of an operating lease, the remaining cost of the lease is considered to be the total lease payments, plus all initial direct costs associated with the lease, minus the lease cost already recognized in previous periods.

After the commencement date, the lessee measures the lease liability at the present value of the lease payments that have not yet been made, using the same discount rate that was established at the commencement date.

After the commencement date, the lessee measures the right-of-use asset at the amount of the lease liability, adjusted for the following items:

- Any impairment of the asset
- Prepaid or accrued lease payments
- Any remaining balance of lease incentives received
- Any unamortized initial direct costs

EXAMPLE

Hinklesville Family Restaurants enters into a 10-year operating lease for restaurant and storage space. The annual lease payment is $40,000 to be paid at the end of each year. The firm incurs initial direct costs of $8,000, and receives $15,000 from the lessor as a lease incentive. Hinklesville's incremental borrowing rate is 6%. The initial direct costs and lease incentive will be amortized over the 10 years of the lease term.

Hinklesville measures the lease liability as the present value of the 10 lease payments at a 6% discount rate, which is $294,404. The right-of-use asset is measured at $287,404, which is the initial $294,404 measurement, plus the initial direct costs of $8,000, minus the lease incentive of $15,000.

After one year, the carrying amount of the lease liability is $272,068, which is the present value of the remaining nine lease payments at a 6% discount rate. The carrying amount of the right-of-use asset is $265,768, which is the amount of the liability, plus the unamortized initial direct costs of $7,200, minus the remaining balance of the lease incentive of $13,500.

Optional Lease Payments

When there is an optional payment in a lease agreement that can be made by the lessee to purchase a leased asset, this optional payment is only included in the recognition of assets and liabilities if it is reasonably certain that the lessee will exercise the purchase option.

Right-of-Use Asset Impairment

If a right-of-use asset is determined to be impaired, the impairment is immediately recorded, thereby reducing the carrying amount of the asset. Its subsequent measurement is calculated as the carrying amount immediately after the impairment transaction, minus any subsequent accumulated amortization.

EXAMPLE

Frog's Legs French Cuisine enters into a five-year equipment lease that is classified as an operating lease. At the end of Year 2, when the carrying amount of the lease liability and the right-of-use asset are both $100,000, the accountant determines that the asset is impaired, and recognizes an impairment loss of $70,000. This reduces the carrying amount of the asset to $30,000.

Beginning in Year 3 and continuing through the remainder of the lease term, Frog's amortizes the right-of-use asset at a rate of $10,000 per year, which will bring the carrying amount of the asset to zero by the end of the lease term.

Derecognition

At the termination of a lease, the right-of-use asset and associated lease liability are removed from the books. The difference between the two amounts is accounted for as a profit or loss at that time. If the lessee purchases the underlying asset at the termination of a lease, then any difference between the purchase price and the lease liability is recorded as an adjustment to the asset's carrying amount.

If a lessee subleases an underlying asset and the terms of the original agreement then relieve the lessee of the primary lease obligation, this is considered a termination of the original lease.

Restaurant and Bar Revenues

The recognition of revenue within a restaurant or bar is dominated by guest checks, which are described within this section. We also note several other revenue-related topics, such as house accounts, coupons, and gift cards.

Guest Checks

A *guest check* is a detailed listing of all the menu items ordered by a customer. This information may be taken down on a paper form, or it may be stored electronically in a point of sale (POS) system. This is an essential source document for the generation of revenue. The main variations on the concept are as follows:

- *Single-part guest check.* In its simplest format, a server writes down a customer's order on a single-part guest check. This form is then sent to the bar or kitchen for fulfillment, after which it is sent back to the server. At the end of the meal, the server uses the guest check as the bill.
- *Two-part guest check.* This is the same as a single-part guest check, except that a second copy is made. The original goes to the kitchen or bar for fulfillment, while the server retains the copy. These two copies are reconciled at the end of the day, to ensure that sales were recorded for all fulfilled orders.
- *Point of sale systems.* This is the same as a two-part guest check, except that there is no paper. Instead, the server punches the order into the system, which then transmits the order to a display screen in the bar and/or kitchen.

Guest Check Payments

A restaurant or bar may take payment only in cash. This approach works best for low-priced, high-volume food service operations, such as food carts or food trucks. For cash sales, a cash register is useful, since the cash drawer secures all cash, while a paper tape records all transactions, and an internal cumulative register total can be compared to daily cash receipts as a control point. The more advanced cash registers can compute sales tax, identify discounts and voids, separately report food and beverage sales, and more.

House Accounts

A *house account* allows a customer to buy meals and drinks on credit. These accounts are most commonly used when a customer is using a restaurant or bar for business meetings, and so routinely piles up large guest checks. House accounts may also be extended to customers who have forgotten their wallets. For these accounts, the restaurant records an immediate sale, with an offsetting debit to the accounts receivable account. If the firm has large house account balances outstanding, it may need to set up an allowance for doubtful accounts, to recognize any expected bad debt losses.

Coupons

Restaurants routinely issue coupons in an effort to increase sales. When customers submit a coupon as part of their payment for a meal, you should record the gross amount of the meal in the sales account, while recording the coupon as a sales discount (which is a contra revenue account).

EXAMPLE

A customer submits a 20% off coupon when paying for an $80 meal. The resulting entry is as follows:

	Debit	Credit
Cash (asset)	64	
Sales discount (contra revenue)	16	
Sales (revenue)		80

Gift Cards

A restaurant may sell gift cards, on the grounds that they provide an immediate cash inflow, and also bring the restaurant to the attention of the card recipients, which may trigger additional sales. However, you do not record a sale transaction when a gift card is sold. Instead, the card sale creates a liability, which is only converted into a sale when the card recipient eventually comes into the restaurant and uses it.

Restaurant and Bar Expenses

There are many expenses that a restaurant or bar may incur, though only a few of them are unique to the industry, or at least have certain unique aspects. We deal with the more industry-specific of these expenses in the following sub-sections.

Cost of Food Sold

Most organizations report a cost of goods sold, but this is modified in the restaurant world to the cost of food sold. This expense contains the cost of all meals incurred by the restaurant, with the exception of the cost of any meals served to employees (see the later Employee Meals Expense item). The amount of this expense can be calculated as follows:

Beginning inventory + Purchases – Ending inventory – Cost of employee meals
= Cost of food sold

Cost of Beverages Sold

The cost of beverages sold may be reported separately from the cost of food sold. This is quite common, since alcoholic beverages are sold at high margins, making beverage sales potentially more profitable than food sales. The following formula is used to determine the amount of this expense:

Beginning inventory + Purchases – Ending inventory
– Transfers from bar + Transfers to bar

= Cost of beverages sold

Employee Meals Expense

Many restaurants provide their employees with free meals. When this is the case, the cost of the meals is considered to be an employee benefit, rather than a cost of food sold. Consequently, it should be shifted out of the cost of sales and into the employee meals expense.

Expendable Items

A restaurant invests a significant amount in china, silverware and linens[3]. While it is possible to capitalize these costs and depreciate them over a short period of time, a more conservative practice is to charge them to expense as incurred.

Franchise Fees

Some restaurant owners prefer the comparative security of franchising a known restaurant brand and business concept. By entering into a franchise agreement, you are agreeing to pay a percentage of your monthly sales to the franchisor. The franchisee may confront several accounting issues that are unique to the franchising process, which are addressed in this sub-section.

Initial Franchise Fees

When a franchisee pays a franchise fee to a franchisor, this payment can be considered an intangible asset. It is permissible for the franchisee to recognize this cost as an asset, since it is an asset acquired from a third party. The franchisee should amortize

---

[3] China, silverware, linens, glassware, pots and pans, tabletop items, bar supplies, food preparation utensils, and low-cost appliances may all be referred to as smallwares.

this asset over its estimated useful life, which is presumed to be the term of the franchise agreement.

EXAMPLE

Furtive Development enters into a franchise arrangement with Bigelow Burgers, paying an upfront fee of $50,000. Furtive records the payment as follows:

	Debit	Credit
Franchise fee (asset)	50,000	
Cash (asset)		50,000

The franchise agreement has a term of 10 years, so Furtive amortizes the fee over 10 years on a straight-line basis. The first-year entry to record this amortization is:

	Debit	Credit
Amortization expense (expense)	5,000	
Accumulated amortization (contra asset)		5,000

This intangible asset should be tested for impairment at least annually. If the carrying amount of the asset exceeds its fair value, write the remaining balance down to its fair value. In the assessment of impairment, review all events and circumstances that could affect the determination of fair value, such as:

- Increases in costs that could negatively impact earnings and cash flows
- Declines in actual or planned revenue
- Regulatory, legal, contractual and other factors that limit fair value
- Litigation
- Management changes or the loss of key personnel
- Decline in the business environment or general economic conditions

EXAMPLE

After three years, Furtive Development has still not constructed the burger franchise location that it is entitled to construct under its franchise agreement with Bigelow Burgers, due to the intractability of the local zoning board in granting a zoning waiver to Furtive. Management concludes that there is no reasonable probability of ever being able to do so, resulting in the write-off of the remaining $35,000 of the franchise fee asset. The related journal entry is:

	Debit	Credit
Impairment loss (expense)	35,000	
Accumulated impairment losses (contra asset)		35,000

Furtive's accountant then removes the franchise fee asset from the firm's accounting records with the following entry:

	Debit	Credit
Accumulated impairment losses (contra asset)	35,000	
Accumulated amortization (contra asset)	15,000	
Franchise fee (asset)		50,000

Franchise Renewal Fees

A franchisee may be required to pay a renewal fee to extend the term of the original franchise agreement. The accounting for this fee is the same as was used for the initial franchise fee.

Payment of Transfer Fee

A franchisee may sell out to a replacement franchisee, which typically calls for the payment of a transfer fee to the franchisor. The outgoing franchisee can account for this fee as a cost of selling the business, which is therefore deducted from the gross proceeds of the sale.

Insurance Expense

All businesses likely incur some type of insurance expense, but restaurants and bars are among the few entities that also acquire liquor liability insurance. This insurance can help cover claims of bodily injury or property damage that an intoxicated customer causes after a restaurant or bar serves them alcohol. This can be very expensive insurance.

Mandatory Gratuity Charges

Some restaurants include a mandatory gratuity charge in the billings presented to their customers. The Internal Revenue Service considers these charges to be service charges rather than tips, because customers no longer have the ability to determine the gratuity amount paid. When this mandatory gratuity is paid over to the restaurant staff, the disbursed amounts are considered to be wages, and so are subject to withholding tax.

Music Licensing Fees

If you plan to play recorded music in your restaurant or bar, you will need to obtain a music license from a music licensing agency. These agencies sell licenses that will allow you to play songs without obtaining any further permission from them. This is an annual fee. There are exemptions from this fee under certain circumstances.

Social Media Promotions

A social media group may contact a restaurant to set up a promotion. For example, the social media group may propose an arrangement where the restaurant offers 50% off its standard menu prices to the members of the social media group, while also paying a promotional fee to the media group. The restaurant should account for these arrangements as a deferred sale (a liability) until the promotional period is over. At the end of the promotional period, and depending on the applicable state laws, any remaining unused coupons may need to be reclassified as a gift card liability.

EXAMPLE

Valley Steakhouse enters into a promotional deal with the CheapDealz social media group, under which the group sells 100 coupons that provide the purchasers with a $50 meal for the low price of $25, and also charges a 20% fee for this service. At the termination date of the promotion, 20 of the coupons have not been used. This results in the following cash flows:

Cash paid by social media group members	$2,500
Minus media group fee	-500
Net payment to Valley Steakhouse	$2,000

Valley's accountant uses the following entry to record the initial transaction:

	Debit	Credit
Cash (asset)	2,000	
Marketing expense (expense)	500	
Social media discount (liability)		2,500

As of the mid-point of the promotion, Valley receives coupons for meals worth $1,000. The accountant records the following entry:

	Debit	Credit
Social media discount (liability)	500	
Sales discount (contra revenue)	500	
Sales (revenue)		1,000

At the termination date of the promotion, $100 of coupons have still not been redeemed. The accountant records the following entry to shift the remaining coupon liability over to the firm's gift card liability account:

	Debit	Credit
Social media discount (liability)	100	
Gift card liability (liability)		100

Third-Party Delivery Fees

Customers are more frequently using third-party delivery apps to have food delivered to their homes from restaurants. The fees charged to restaurants are significant, so how they are accounted for bears some examination. There are several viable approaches, which are as follows:

- Net the delivery fee against sales, so that the total revenue recognized is lowered by the amount of the delivery fee. For example, a $75 customer order with a $10 delivery fee would be recorded as a sale of $65.
- Record the full customer order amount, and record the delivery fee as a marketing expense. For example, the same $75 customer order would be recorded as a $75 sale, along with a $10 marketing expense.
- Record the full customer order amount, and record the delivery fee as a cost of sales. For example, the same $75 customer order would be recorded as a $75 sale, along with a $10 cost of sales.

All three approaches are valid, since they all result in the same reported net profit. However, the first option results in a lower reported sales level, while the second option results in an inflated gross margin, and the third option results in a reduced gross margin. In the author's opinion, the third option represents the best portrayal of revenues earned and the nature of the expense being incurred.

Website Development Costs

A restaurant or bar may allocate funds to the development of a company website in such areas as coding, graphics design, the addition of content, and site operation. The accounting for website development varies, depending upon the stage of completion of the project. The relevant accounting is:

- *Stage 1: Preliminary.* Charge all site planning costs to expense as incurred. This stage is considered to include project planning, the determination of site functionality, hardware identification, technology usability, alternatives analysis, supplier demonstrations, and legal considerations.
- *Stage 2: Application development and infrastructure.* These costs are capitalized. More specifically, capitalize the cost of obtaining and registering an Internet domain, as well as the procurement of software tools, code customization, web page development, related hardware, hypertext link creation, and site testing. Also, if a site upgrade provides new functions or features to the website, capitalize these costs.
- *Stage 3: Graphics development.* For the purposes of this topic, graphics are considered to be software and so are capitalized, unless they are to be marketed externally. Graphics development includes site page design and layout.
- *Stage 4: Content development.* Charge data conversion costs to expense as incurred, as well as the costs to input content into a website. Content may include articles, photos, maps, charts, and so forth.

- *Stage 5: Site operation.* The costs to operate a website are the same as any other operating costs, and so should be charged to expense as incurred. Operating costs relate to training, administration, site updates, site security, and maintenance. The treatment of selected operating costs associated with a website are:
  - o Charge website hosting fees to expense over the period benefited by the hosting
  - o Charge search engine registration fees to expense as incurred, since they are advertising costs

Accounting for Payroll

There are several types of journal entries that involve the recordation of compensation for a restaurant or bar. The primary entry is for the initial recordation of a payroll. This entry records the gross wages earned by employees, as well as all withholdings from their pay, and any additional taxes owed by the entity. There may also be an accrued wages entry that is recorded at the end of each accounting period, and which is intended to record the amount of wages owed to employees but not yet paid. Each of these types of compensation is based on different source documents and requires separate calculations and journal entries.

There are also a number of other payroll-related journal entries that you must deal with on a regular basis. They include:

- Tips and tip credits
- Manual paychecks
- Accrued vacation pay
- Tax deposits

All of these journal entries are described in the following subsections.

Primary Payroll Journal Entry

The primary journal entry for payroll is the summary-level entry that is compiled from the payroll register, and which is recorded in either the payroll journal or the general ledger. This entry usually includes debits for the direct labor expense, wages, and the employer's portion of payroll taxes. There will also be credits to a number of other accounts, each one detailing the liability for payroll taxes that have not been paid, as well as for the amount of cash already paid to employees for their net pay. The basic entry (assuming no further breakdown of debits by individual profit center) appears in the following exhibit.

Recordation of Basic Payroll

	Debit	Credit
Compensation expense (expense)	xxx	
Payroll taxes expense (expense)	xxx	
Cash (asset)		xxx
Federal withholding taxes payable (liability)		xxx
Social security taxes payable (liability)		xxx
Medicare taxes payable (liability)		xxx
Federal unemployment taxes payable (liability)		xxx
State unemployment taxes payable (liability)		xxx
Garnishments payable (liability)		xxx

The reason for the payroll taxes expense line item in this journal entry is that the employer incurs the cost of matching the social security and Medicare amounts paid by employees, and directly incurs the cost of unemployment insurance. The employee-paid portions of the social security and Medicare taxes are not recorded as expenses; instead, they are liabilities for which the employer has an obligation to remit cash to the taxing government entity.

A key point with this journal entry is that the compensation expense contains employee gross pay, while the amount actually paid to employees through the cash account is their net pay. The difference between the two figures (which can be substantial) is the amount of deductions from their pay, such as payroll taxes and withholdings to pay for benefits.

There may be a number of additional employee deductions to include in this journal entry. For example, there may be deductions for 401(k) pension plans, health insurance, life insurance, vision insurance, and for the repayment of advances.

When the withheld taxes and employer portion of payroll taxes are paid on a later date, use the entry format in the following exhibit to reduce the balance in the cash account, and eliminate the balances in the liability accounts.

Recordation of Payroll Tax Payments

	Debit	Credit
Federal withholding taxes payable (liability)	xxx	
Social security taxes payable (liability)	xxx	
Medicare taxes payable (liability)	xxx	
Federal unemployment taxes payable (liability)	xxx	
State withholding taxes payable (liability)	xxx	
State unemployment taxes payable (liability)	xxx	
Garnishments payable (liability)	xxx	
Cash (asset)		xxx

Thus, when an employer initially deducts taxes and other items from an employee's pay, it incurs a liability to pay the taxes to a third party. This liability only disappears from its accounting records when it pays the related funds to the entity to which they are owed.

Tip Distribution Systems

Some restaurants use tip sharing or tip pooling systems. Under a tip sharing system, employees can keep a portion of the tips they earn, while sharing a portion of their earnings with other restaurant employees – such as bartenders or bussers. Tip sharing is conducted at the discretion of each tipped employee, to encourage other staff to prioritize activities that will earn more tips. For example, a server might share tips with a busser in order to encourage the busser to clean the server's tables faster, which allows the server to cycle through more customers and thereby earn more money.

A different approach is tip pooling, where all tips collected by employees are combined and then distributed amongst the group, irrespective of their individual performance. Collecting and distributing these tips can put pressure on the restaurant manager, especially when there are many employees working each shift. This is even more difficult when employee start and stop times carry over across different shifts. However, it can be useful to operate a tip pool when there is a large pay disparity between some of the positions within a restaurant.

A good tip distribution system interfaces directly with a restaurant's payroll system, so that tips are included in the total reported compensation of employees.

Tip Credit

Under current federal law, the minimum wage is $7.25 per hour. A restaurant or bar employer can satisfy this payment obligation by paying a base rate of $2.13 and paying the remaining $5.12 per hour through the value of the tips received by employees.

Tip credits allow an employer to credit a portion of an employee's tips toward the employer's obligation to pay minimum wage. These credits can only be applied to a tipped employee, which is someone who regularly earns at least $30 per month in tips, and it can only be applied to those hours of work that produce tips or directly support tip-producing work. Tips can come directly from customers, or they may be distributed as part of a tip pool.

When the employer takes a tip credit, the tips earned by an employee must equal at least the difference between their direct cash wage and the minimum wage for the jurisdiction in which the employee works. The employer is required to make up the difference if the employee's combined wages (of direct cash wages and tips) do not attain the minimum wage level.

Non-tipped employees do not qualify for the tip credit, so the employer must pay these people at least the minimum wage for all hours worked. This means that those employees in the usual serving occupations – wait staff, bartenders, bussers, and so forth – qualify for the tip credit, while those working in the kitchen do not.

Tips

In general, any tips that employees receive from customers are treated as taxable income[4]. Employees are required to report cash tips to the employer by the tenth day of the month after the month in which they received the tips, but not if the tips received were less than $20. This report should include:

- Tips forwarded by the company to employees that were paid with charge cards
- Tips employees received directly from customers
- Tips distributed from a tip-sharing arrangement

Employees report tips to the restaurant on Form 4070, *Employee's Report of Tips to Employer*. It is also allowable to create a similar form or an electronic system for employees to use. Such forms or systems must contain exactly the same information that would otherwise be reported on Form 4070, as well as the employee's signature (an electronic signature is acceptable if an electronic reporting system is used). Any electronic system must be capable of producing a hard copy, in case the IRS audits tip income.

The employer is responsible for collecting taxes from employee wages for reported tips, and for providing the employer-matched amounts for applicable taxes. If there are not enough employee funds available from which to deduct taxes by the tenth day of the month after the month for which tips are being reported, the employer is no longer responsible for collecting any remaining taxes. Where there are not sufficient funds, the employer should withhold taxes in the following order:

1. Withhold on regular wages (not tips); then
2. Withhold social security and Medicare taxes on tips; then
3. Withhold income taxes on tips.

If the employer is unable to collect some taxes, report the uncollected amounts of social security and Medicare taxes in Box 12 of Form W-2.

---

[4] As noted in IRS Publication 15, *Employer's Tax Guide*, Tips

EXAMPLE

Andrew Malone is a waiter at the Crumb Cake Café. He reports $400 in tip income for the preceding month. In addition, Crumb Cake paid him $100 in hourly wages. His wage and tax withholding situation is:

	Wage Income	Tip Income	Total Income
Gross pay	$100.00	$400.00	$500.00
Federal income tax	(20.00)	(80.00)	(100.00)
Social security	(6.20)	(24.80)	(31.00)
Medicare	(1.45)	(5.80)	(7.25)
Total withholdings	$(27.65)	$(110.60)	$(138.25)
Net pay	$72.35	$289.40	$361.75

Crumb Cake's accountant determines that the total withholdings required for Mr. Malone, according to the preceding table, amount to $138.25, and yet the company is only paying him $100 from which to withhold the funds. Thus, the accountant uses the following progression of deductions to reach the $100 maximum withholding:

Priority	Items to Withhold	Withheld	Funds Remaining
1	Withholdings on wages	$(27.65)	$72.35
2	Social security and Medicare on tip income	(30.60)	41.75
3	Income taxes on tip income	41.75	0

The preceding table shows that only $41.75 of income taxes can be withheld from Mr. Malone's tip income, rather than the $80.00 that should be withheld. Mr. Malone is responsible for the $38.25 shortfall.

Tips Charged to Credit Cards

Most tips are included on customer credit card charges. A restaurant may pay these charged tips to employees at the end of the shift. If so, it takes the necessary funds from cash. For example, a restaurant generates $5,000 in credit card receivables, of which $4,000 is sales and the remaining $1,000 is tips. The journal entry would be:

	Debit	Credit
Accounts receivable – credit cards (asset)	5,000	
Sales (revenue)		4,000
Cash (asset)		1,000

Alternatively, if the restaurant elects to pay tips to employees as part of their next paycheck, then the following entry would be used instead:

	Debit	Credit
Accounts receivable – credit cards (asset)	5,000	
Sales (revenue)		4,000
Payable to employees (liability)		1,000

Accrued Wages

It is quite common to have some amount of unpaid wages at the end of an accounting period, so accrue this expense (if it is material). The accrual entry, as shown next, is simpler than the comprehensive payroll entry already shown, because all payroll taxes are typically clumped into a single expense account and offsetting liability account. After recording this entry, reverse it at the beginning of the following accounting period, and then record the actual payroll expense whenever it occurs.

	Debit	Credit
Wages expense (expense)	xxx	
Accrued salaries and wages (liability)		xxx
Accrued payroll taxes (liability)		xxx

The information for the wage accrual entry is most easily derived from a spreadsheet that itemizes all employees to whom the calculation applies, the amount of unpaid time, and the standard pay rate for each person. It is not necessary to also calculate the cost of overtime hours earned during an accrual period if the amount of such hours is relatively small. A sample spreadsheet for calculating accrued wages appears in the following exhibit.

Sample Accrued Wages Calculation

Hourly Employees	Unpaid Days	Hourly Rate	Pay Accrual
Anthem, Jill	4	$20.00	$640
Bingley, Adam	4	18.25	584
Chesterton, Elvis	4	17.50	560
Davis, Ethel	4	23.00	736
Ellings, Humphrey	4	21.50	688
Fogarty, Miriam	4	26.00	832
		Total	$4,040

Manual Paycheck Entry

It is all too common to create a manual paycheck, either because an employee was short-paid in a prior payroll, or because the employer is laying off or firing an employee, and so is obligated to pay that person before the next regularly scheduled payroll. This check may be paid through the employer's accounts payable bank account, rather than its payroll account, so you may need to make this entry through the accounts payable system.

EXAMPLE

Emilio's Mexican Restaurant lays off Mr. Jones. It owes Mr. Jones $5,000 of wages at the time of the layoff. The accountant calculates that she must withhold $382.50 from Mr. Jones' pay to cover the employee-paid portions of social security and Medicare taxes. Mr. Jones has claimed a large enough number of withholding allowances that there is no income tax withholding. Thus, the accountant pays Mr. Jones $4,617.50. The journal entry used is:

	Debit	Credit
Wage expense (expense)	5,000	
Social security taxes payable (liability)		310.00
Medicare taxes payable (liability)		72.50
Cash (asset)		4,617.50

At the next regularly-scheduled payroll, the accountant records this payment as a notation in the payroll system, so that it will properly compile the correct amount of wages for Mr. Jones for his year-end Form W-2. In addition, the payroll system calculates that the restaurant must pay a matching amount of social security and Medicare taxes (though no unemployment taxes, since Mr. Jones already exceeded his wage cap for these taxes). Accordingly, an additional liability of $382.50 is recorded in the payroll journal entry for that payroll. The restaurant pays these matching amounts as part of its normal tax remittances associated with the payroll.

Accrued Vacation Pay

Accrued vacation pay is the amount of vacation time that an employee has earned as per an employer's employee benefit manual, but which he or she has not yet used. The calculation of accrued vacation pay for each employee is:

1. Calculate the amount of vacation time earned through the beginning of the accounting period. This should be a roll-forward balance from the preceding period.
2. Add the number of hours earned in the current accounting period.
3. Subtract the number of vacation hours used in the current period.
4. Multiply the ending number of accrued vacation hours by the employee's hourly wage to arrive at the correct accrual that should be on the restaurant's books.

5. If the amount already accrued for the employee from the preceding period is lower than the correct accrual, record the difference as an addition to the accrued liability. If the amount already accrued from the preceding period is higher than the correct accrual, record the difference as a reduction of the accrued liability.

A sample spreadsheet follows that uses the preceding steps, and which can be used to compile accrued vacation pay.

Sample Accrued Vacation Spreadsheet

Name	Vacation Roll-Forward Balance	+ New Hours Earned	- Hours Used	= Net Balance	× Hourly Pay	= Accrued Vacation $
Hilton, David	24.0	10	34.0	0.0	$25.00	$0.00
Idle, John	13.5	10	0.0	23.5	27.50	646.25
Jakes, Jill	120.0	10	80.0	50.0	23.50	1,175.00
Kilo, Steve	114.5	10	14.0	110.5	20.00	2,210.00
Linder, Alice	12.0	10	0.0	22.0	25.75	566.50
Mills, Jeffery	83.5	10	65.00	28.5	29.75	847.88
					Total	$5,445.63

It is not necessary to reverse the vacation pay accrual in each period if the decision is made to instead record just incremental changes in the accrual from month to month.

EXAMPLE

There is already an existing accrued balance of 40 hours of unused vacation time for Wes Smith on the books of Kent Seafood. In the most recent month that has just ended, Mr. Smith accrued an additional five hours of vacation time (since he is entitled to 60 hours of accrued vacation time per year, and $60 \div 12$ = five hours per month). He also used three hours of vacation time during the month. This means that, as of the end of the month, the accountant should have accrued a total of 42 hours of vacation time for him (calculated as 40 hours existing balance + 5 hours additional accrual – 3 hours used).

Mr. Smith is paid $30 per hour, so his total vacation accrual should be $1,260 (42 hours × $30/hour), so the accountant accrues an additional $60 of vacation liability.

What if a restaurant or bar has a "use it or lose it" policy? This means that employees must use their vacation time by a certain date (such as the end of the year), and can only carry forward a small number of hours (if any) into the next year. One issue is that this policy may be illegal, since vacation is an earned benefit that cannot be taken away (which depends on state law). If this policy is considered to be legal, it is acceptable to reduce the accrual as of the date when employees are supposed to have used their accrued vacation, thereby reflecting the reduced liability to the restaurant or bar as represented by the number of vacation hours that employees have lost.

What if an employee receives a pay raise? Then increase the amount of his entire vacation accrual by the incremental amount of the pay raise. This is because, if the employee were to leave the business and be paid all of his unused vacation pay, he would be paid at his most recent rate of pay.

Tax Deposits

When an employer withholds taxes from employee pay, it must deposit these funds with the government at stated intervals. The journal entry for doing so is a debit to the tax liability account being paid and a credit to the cash account, which reduces the cash balance. The following exhibit shows the entry needed if a restaurant or bar were to pay a state government for unemployment taxes.

Recordation of State Unemployment Tax Payment

	Debit	Credit
State unemployment taxes payable (liability)	1,000	
Cash (asset)		1,000

Accounting for Sales Taxes

A *sales tax* is a tax imposed on the sale of tangible personal property and certain services, and is calculated as a percentage of the sales price. The tax is collected by the entity selling the property to a third party, and is remitted to the applicable government entity at regular intervals. The most common arrangement is to have *state-collected taxes*, where all sales taxes are sent to a state's Department of Revenue, which retains the state portion of each tax and then distributes the remainder to the applicable county and city governments and special taxation districts. *Home-rule* or *self-collected* counties, cities, and special taxation districts mandate that those collecting sales taxes remit the taxes directly to them (which greatly increases the volume of required sales tax reporting).

From the perspective of a restaurant, the food cost of a free meal may be subject to sales tax, as may any automatic gratuities charged to customers. Also, any merchandise sales will likely be subject to sales tax. Many bars are required to pay sales tax on their liquor sales.

EXAMPLE

The city of Lakewood, Colorado has an overall 7.5% sales tax, which is derived from the following types of sales taxes:

Jurisdiction	Rate
Colorado sales tax	2.9%
Jefferson County sales tax	0.5%
Lakewood sales tax	3.0%
Special district sales tax (two special districts are involved)	1.1%
Total sales tax	7.5%

A person purchases $200 of taxable goods from a restaurant within the city limits of Lakewood and is charged a 7.5% sales tax for a total charge of $215.00. Of the $15.00 of sales tax charged to the person, Colorado receives $5.80 ($200 × 2.9%), Jefferson County receives $1.00 ($200 × 0.5%), the city of Lakewood receives $6.00 ($200 × 3.0%), and the special districts receive $2.20 ($200 × 1.1%).

When a customer is charged for sales taxes, the journal entry is a debit to the cash account for the combined amount of the sale and the related sales tax, a credit to the sales account for that portion of the transaction attributable to taxable goods or services, and a credit to the sales tax liability account for the amount of sales taxes associated with the transaction.

At the end of the month (or longer, depending on the remittance arrangement with the state), the accountant fills out a sales tax remittance form that states gross sales and sales taxes and sends the government the amount of the sales tax recorded in the sales tax liability account.

EXAMPLE

International Restaurants is paid $1,000 for taxable goods sold, on which there is a seven percent sales tax. The entry is:

	Debit	Credit
Cash (asset)	1,070	
Sales (revenue)		1,000
Sales tax liability (liability)		70

Following the end of the month, International remits the sales taxes withheld to the state government. The entry is:

	Debit	Credit
Sales tax liability (liability)	70	
Cash (asset)		70

A few states allow a business to retain a small portion of its sales tax collections as a discount. This discount is only made available if the firm remits payments on a timely basis.

Closing the Books

The concept of closing the books refers to summarizing the information in the accounting records into the financial statements at the end of a reporting period. In this section, we give an overview of closing journal entries and the most prevalent closing activities that a restaurant or bar is likely to need.

Adjusting Entries

Adjusting entries are journal entries that are used at the end of an accounting period to adjust the balances in various general ledger accounts to more closely align the reported results and financial position of a business to meet the requirements of an accounting framework, such as Generally Accepted Accounting Principles.

An adjusting entry can be used for any type of accounting transaction; here are some of the more common ones:

- To record depreciation
- To record accrued expenses
- To record previously paid but unused expenditures as prepaid expenses
- To adjust cash balances for any reconciling items noted in the bank reconciliation

Adjusting entries are most commonly of three types, which are:

- *Accruals*. To record a revenue or expense that has not yet been recorded through a standard accounting transaction.
- *Deferrals*. To defer a revenue or expense that has occurred, but which has not yet been earned or used.
- *Estimates*. To estimate the amount of a reserve, such as for spoiled food inventory.

When a journal entry is recorded for an accrual, deferral, or estimate, it usually impacts an asset or liability account. For example, if an expense is accrued, this also increases a liability account. Or, if revenue recognition is deferred to a later period, this also increases a liability account. Thus, adjusting entries impact the balance sheet, not just the income statement.

Reversing Entries

When a journal entry is created, it may be to record revenue or an expense other than through a more traditional method, such as issuing an invoice to a banquet customer or recording an invoice from a supplier. In these situations, the journal entry is only meant to be a stopgap measure, with the traditional recordation method still being used at a later date. This means that the accountant has to eventually create a journal entry that is the *opposite* of the original entry, thereby cancelling out the original entry. The concept is best explained with an example.

EXAMPLE

The accountant of Sam's Seafood has not yet received an invoice from a key supplier by the time he closes the books for the month of May. He expects that the invoice will be for $2,000, so he records the following accrual entry for the invoice:

	Debit	Credit
Repairs expense (expense)	2,000	
Accrued expenses (liability)		2,000

This entry creates an additional expense of $2,000 for the month of May.

The accountant knows that the invoice will arrive in June and will be recorded upon receipt. Therefore, he creates a reversing entry for the original accrual in early June that cancels out the original entry. The entry is:

	Debit	Credit
Accrued expenses (liability)	2,000	
Repairs expense (expense)		2,000

The invoice then arrives, and is recorded in the normal manner through the accounts payable module in Sam's accounting software. This creates an expense during the month of June of $2,000. Thus, the net effect in June is:

June reversing entry	-$2,000
Supplier invoice	+2,000
Net effect in June	$0

In short, the accrual entry shifts recognition of the expense from June to May.

Any accounting software package contains an option for automatically creating a reversing journal entry when a journal entry is initially set up. Always use this feature when a reversing entry will be needed. By doing so, you can avoid the risk of forgetting to manually create the reversing entry, and also avoid the risk of creating an incorrect entry.

> **Tip:** There will be situations where there is no expectation to reverse a journal entry for a few months. If so, consider using an automated reversing entry in the *next* month, and creating a replacement journal entry in each successive month. While this approach may appear time-consuming, it ensures that the original entry is *always* flushed from the books, thereby avoiding the risk of carrying a journal entry past the date when it should have been eliminated.

Common Adjusting Entries

This section contains a discussion of the journal entries that a restaurant or bar is most likely to need to close the books, along with an example of the accounts most likely to be used in the entries.

Depreciation

This entry is used to gradually charge the investment in fixed assets to expense over the useful lives of those assets. The amount of depreciation is calculated from a spreadsheet or fixed asset software, and is based on a systematic method for spreading recognition of the expense over multiple periods. This entry was already described earlier in the book.

Accrued Expenses

If there are supplier invoices that you are aware of but have not yet received, estimate the amount of the expense and accrue it with a journal entry. There are any number of expense accounts to which such transactions might be charged; in the following sample entry, we assume that the expense relates to a supplier invoice for utilities that has not yet arrived.

	Debit	Credit
Utilities expense (expense)	xxx	
Accrued expenses (liability)		xxx

This is likely to be the most frequent of the adjusting entries, as there may be a number of supplier invoices that do not arrive by the time you officially close the books.

Prepaid Expenses

Occasionally, you will make a significant payment in advance to a third party. This advance may be for something that will be charged to expense in a later period, or it may be a deposit that will be returned at a later date. These payments should initially be recorded as assets, usually in the prepaid expenses account. Situations where one may record a prepaid expense include:

- Rent paid before the month to which it applies
- Medical insurance paid before the month to which it applies
- Rent deposit, to be returned at the conclusion of a lease
- Utilities deposit, to be retained until the organization cancels service

Most of these transactions have the same journal entry, which is:

	Debit	Credit
Prepaid expenses (liability)	xxx	
Cash (asset)		xxx

The name of the debited account can vary. We use "Prepaid expenses" in the sample entry, but "Prepaid assets" is also used.

Reconcile the Bank Statement

The bank reconciliation matches the amount of cash recorded by the business to what its bank has recorded. Once a bank reconciliation has been constructed, you can have considerable confidence that the amount of cash appearing on the balance sheet is correct.

At a minimum, conduct a bank reconciliation shortly after the end of each month, when the bank sends a bank statement containing the bank's beginning cash balance, transactions during the month, and its ending cash balance. It is even better to conduct a bank reconciliation every day based on the bank's month-to-date information, which should be accessible on the bank's web site. By completing a daily bank reconciliation, problems can be spotted and corrected immediately.

A likely outcome of the reconciliation process will be several adjustments to your recorded cash balance. It is unlikely that the firm's ending cash balance and the bank's ending cash balance will be identical, since there are probably multiple payments and deposits in transit at all times, as well as bank service fees, penalties, and not sufficient funds deposits that you have not yet recorded.

The essential process flow for a bank reconciliation is to start with the bank's ending cash balance (known as the *bank balance*), add to it any deposits in transit from the business to the bank, subtract any checks that have not yet cleared the bank, and either add or deduct any other reconciling items. Then find the firm's ending cash balance and deduct from it any bank service fees, not sufficient funds (NSF) checks and penalties, and add to it any interest earned. At the end of this process, the adjusted bank balance should equal the firm's ending adjusted cash balance.

The following bank reconciliation procedure assumes that the bank reconciliation is being created in an accounting software package, which makes the reconciliation process easier:

1. Enter the bank reconciliation software module. A listing of uncleared checks and uncleared deposits will appear.
2. Check off in the bank reconciliation module all checks that are listed on the bank statement as having cleared the bank.
3. Check off in the bank reconciliation module all deposits that are listed on the bank statement as having cleared the bank.
4. Enter as expenses all bank charges appearing on the bank statement, and which have not already been recorded in your records.
5. Enter the ending balance on the bank statement. If the book and bank balances match, then post all changes recorded in the bank reconciliation, and close the module. If the balances do *not* match, then continue reviewing the bank reconciliation for additional reconciling items. Look for the following items:

   - Checks recorded in the bank records at a different amount from what is recorded in the firm's records.
   - Deposits recorded in the bank records at a different amount from what is recorded in the firm's records.
   - Checks recorded in the bank records that are not recorded at all in the firm's records.
   - Deposits recorded in the bank records that are not recorded at all in the firm's records.
   - Inbound wire transfers from which a processing fee has been extracted.

EXAMPLE

Simply Devine Barbecue is closing its books for the month ended April 30. Simply's accountant must prepare a bank reconciliation based on the following issues:

1. The bank statement contains an ending bank balance of $320,000.
2. The bank statement contains a $200 check printing charge for new checks that the firm ordered.
3. The bank statement contains a $150 service charge for operating the bank account.
4. The bank rejected a deposit of $500 due to not sufficient funds, and charges the firm a $10 fee associated with the rejection.
5. The bank statement contains interest income of $30.
6. Simply issued $80,000 of checks that have not yet cleared the bank.
7. Simply deposited $25,000 of checks at month-end that were not deposited in time to appear on the bank statement.

The accountant creates the following reconciliation:

		Item #	Adjustment to Books
Bank balance	$320,000	1	
- Check printing charge	-200	2	Debit expense, credit cash
- Service charge	-150	3	Debit expense, credit cash
- NSF fee	-10	4	Debit expense, credit cash
- NSF deposit rejected	-500	4	Debit receivable, credit cash
+ Interest income	+30	5	Debit cash, credit interest income
- Uncleared checks	-80,000	6	None
+ Deposits in transit	+25,000	7	None
= Book balance	$264,170		

When the bank reconciliation process is complete, print a report through the accounting software that shows the bank and book balances, the identified differences between the two (most likely to be uncleared checks), and any remaining unreconciled difference.

The format of the report will vary by software package; a simplistic layout follows.

Sample Bank Reconciliation Statement

For the month ended March 31, 20x3		
Bank balance	$850,000	
Less: Checks outstanding	-225,000	See detail
Add: Deposits in transit	+100,000	See detail
+/- Other adjustments	0	
Book balance	$725,000	
Unreconciled difference	$0	

There are several problems that continually arise as part of a bank reconciliation. They are:

- *Uncleared checks that continue to not be presented.* There will be a residual number of checks that either are not presented to the bank for payment for a long time, or which are never presented for payment. In the short term, treat them in the same manner as any other uncleared checks - just keep them in the uncleared checks listing in the accounting software, so they will be an ongoing reconciling item. In the long term, contact the payee to see if they ever received the check; it will likely be necessary to void the old check and issue them a new one.
- *Checks clear the bank after having been voided.* As just noted, if a check remains uncleared for a long time, the old check will likely be voided and replaced with a new check. But what if the payee then cashes the original check? If it was voided with the bank, the bank should reject the check when it is presented. If the accountant did *not* void it with the bank, then record the check again in the accounting records, which will reduce the cash balance. If the payee has not yet cashed the replacement check, void it with the bank at once to avoid a double payment. Otherwise, it will be necessary to pursue repayment of the second check by the payee.
- *Deposited checks are returned.* There are cases where the bank will refuse to deposit a check, usually because it is drawn on a bank account located in another country. In this case, reverse the original entry related to that deposit, which will reduce the cash balance.

Record All Payables

Accounts payable can be a significant bottleneck in the closing process. The reason is that some suppliers only issue invoices at the end of each month when they are closing *their* books, so the restaurant or bar will not receive their invoices until several days into the next month. This circumstance usually arises either when a supplier ships something near the end of the month or when it is providing a continuing service. There are several choices for dealing with these items:

1. *Do nothing.* By waiting a few days, the invoices will arrive in the mail, and you can record the invoices and close the books. The advantage of this

approach is a high degree of precision and perfect supporting evidence for all expenses. The downside is that it can significantly delay the issuance of financial statements.

2. *Accrue continuing service items.* As just noted, suppliers providing continuing services are more likely to issue invoices at month-end. When services are being provided on a continuing basis, you can easily estimate what the expense should be, based on prior invoices. Thus, it is not difficult to create reversing journal entries for these items at the end of the month. It is likely that these accruals will vary somewhat from the amounts on the actual invoices, but the differences should be immaterial.

3. *Accrue based on purchase orders.* As just noted, suppliers issue invoices at month-end when they ship goods near that date. If the business is using purchase orders to order these items, the supplier is supposed to issue an invoice containing the same price stated on the purchase order. Therefore, if an item is received at the receiving dock but there is no accompanying invoice, use the purchase order to create a reversing journal entry that accrues the expense associated with the received item.

In short, we strongly recommend using accruals to record expenses for supplier invoices that have not yet arrived. The sole exception is the end of the fiscal year, when the outside auditors may expect a greater degree of precision and supporting evidence, and will expect the accountant to wait for actual invoices to arrive before closing the books.

Reconcile Accounts

It is important to examine the contents of the balance sheet accounts to verify that the recorded assets and liabilities are supposed to be there. It is quite possible that some items are still listed in an account that should have been flushed out a long time ago, which can be quite embarrassing if they are still on record when the auditors review the firm's books at the end of the year. Here are several situations that a proper account reconciliation would have caught:

*   *Prepaid assets.* A restaurant pays $5,000 to an insurance company as an advance on its regular monthly medical insurance, and records the payment as a prepaid asset. The asset lingers on the books until year-end, when the auditors inquire about it, and the full amount is then charged to expense.
*   *Depreciation.* A brewpub calculates the depreciation on many assets with an electronic spreadsheet, which unfortunately does not track when to stop depreciating assets. A year-end review finds that the organization charged $40,000 of excess depreciation to expense.
*   *Accumulated depreciation.* A restaurant has been disposing of its assets for years, but has never bothered to eliminate the associated accumulated depreciation from its balance sheet. Doing so reduces both the fixed asset and accumulated depreciation accounts by 50%.

- *Accounts payable*. A restaurant does not compare its accounts payable detail report to the general ledger account balance, which is $8,000 lower than the detail. The auditors spot the error and require a correcting entry at year-end, so that the account balance matches the detail report.

These issues and many more are common problems encountered at year-end. To prevent the extensive error corrections caused by these problems, conduct account reconciliations every month for the larger accounts, and occasionally review the detail for the smaller accounts, too. The following exhibit contains some of the account reconciliations to conduct, as well as the specific issues for which to look.

Sample Account Reconciliation List

Account	Reconciliation Discussion
Cash	There can be a number of unrecorded checks, deposits, and bank fees that will only be spotted with a bank reconciliation. It is permissible to do a partial bank reconciliation a day or two before the close, but completely ignoring it is not a good idea.
Prepaid expenses	This account may contain a variety of assets that will be charged to expense in the short term, so it may require frequent reviews to ensure that items have been flushed out in a timely manner.
Inventory	Always compare the firm's records for food and liquor on hand to what is actually present, and investigate any differences.
Fixed assets	It is quite likely that fixed assets will initially be recorded in the wrong fixed asset account, or that they are disposed of incorrectly. Reconcile the account to the fixed asset detail report at least once a quarter to spot and correct these issues.
Accumulated depreciation	The balance in this account may not match the fixed asset detail if you have not removed the accumulated depreciation from the account upon the sale or disposal of an asset. This is not a critical issue, but still warrants an occasional review.
Accounts payable	The accounts payable detail report should match the account balance. If not, a journal entry was probably included in the account, which should be reversed.
Accrued expenses	This account can include a large number of accruals for such expenses as wages, vacations, and benefits. It is good practice to reverse all of these expenses in the month following recordation. Thus, if there is a residual balance, there may be an excess accrual still on the books.
Notes payable	The balance in this account should exactly match the account balance of the lender, barring any exceptions for in-transit payments to the lender.

The number of accounts that can be reconciled makes it clear that this is one of the larger steps involved in closing the books. Selected reconciliations can be skipped from time to time, but doing so presents the risk of an error creeping into the financial statements and not being spotted for quite a few months. Consequently, there is a significant risk of issuing inaccurate financial statements if some reconciliations are continually avoided.

Review Financial Statements

Once all of the preceding steps have been completed, review the financial statements for errors. There are several ways to do so, including:

- *Horizontal analysis.* Print reports that show the income statement and balance sheet for the past twelve months on a rolling basis. Track across each line item to see if there are any unusual declines or spikes in comparison to the results of prior periods, and investigate those items. This is the best review technique.
- *Budget versus actual.* Print an income statement that shows budgeted versus actual results, and investigate any larger variances. This is a less effective review technique, because it assumes that the budget is realistic, and also because a budget is not usually available for the balance sheet.

There will almost always be problems with the first iteration of the financial statements. Expect to investigate and correct several items before issuing a satisfactory set of financials. To reduce the amount of time needed to review financial statement errors during the core closing period, consider doing so a few days prior to month-end; this may uncover a few errors, leaving a smaller number to investigate later on.

Accrue Tax Liabilities

Once the financial statements have been created and the information in them has been finalized, there may be a need to accrue an income tax liability based on the amount of net profit. There are several issues to consider when creating this accrual:

- *Income tax rate.* When accruing income taxes, use the average expected income tax rate for the full year.
- *Losses.* If the business has earned a taxable profit in a prior period of the year, and has now generated a loss, accrue for a tax rebate, which will offset the tax expense that was recorded earlier. Doing so creates the correct amount of tax liability when looking at year-to-date results. If there was no prior profit and no reasonable prospect of one, do not accrue for a tax rebate, since it is more likely than not that the firm will not receive the rebate.

Once the income tax liability has been accrued, print the complete set of financial statements.

Close the Month

Once all transactions have been entered into the accounting system, close the month in the accounting software. This means prohibiting any further transactions in the general ledger in the old accounting period, as well as allowing the next accounting period to accept transactions. These steps are important, to avoid inadvertently entering transactions into the wrong accounting periods. Then issue the financial statements.

Restaurant and Bar Cost Controls

An essential element of running a profitable restaurant or bar is cost control. An analysis of restaurant costs usually involves the following four cost classifications:

- *Beverage costs*. This classification is primarily related to the sale of alcoholic drinks, as well as the ingredients needed to produce these drinks (such as mixers, cherries, and olives). Nonalcoholic drinks are generally classified as food items.
- *Food costs*. Includes the costs of dairy, fruits, meats, vegetables, and so forth.
- *Labor costs*. Includes the cost of the staff needed to run the restaurant, as well as the related payroll and benefit costs.
- *Other costs*. Includes china, glassware, pots and pans, linen, rent, utilities, franchise fees, and so forth.

While many cost control actions fall well outside of this accounting book, we do provide the following pointers that have a bearing on the accounting aspects of restaurant operations:

- *Mandate formal meal recipes*. The only accounting issue associated with the use of recipes is whether standard quantities are included in the recipes. They should be, so that you can multiply these standard amounts by the number of menu items prepared, thereby producing a standard unit quantity that can be used in an analysis of food costs.
- *Mandate the use of scales*. Require the kitchen staff to use scales to weigh the more expensive meal ingredients, such as meat or cheese, so that the sizes mandated in recipes are followed. At a minimum, the manager should weigh a selection of meal portions on a test basis.
- *Track food waste*. When analyzing food costs, be sure to factor in the waste percentage, which is the amount of usable food left after a food item has been cleaned, trimmed, and cooked. This could result in a substantial reduction in the actual amount of food being served to customers. Thus, if a customer is promised a four-ounce food item, but you have to start with six ounces of food prior to the preparation process, then the waste is one-third. This is a major factor when analyzing whether food costs are reasonable.
- *Watch for over portioning*. Some restaurant staff may provide customers with excessively large portions. This can drastically increase food costs, especially when over portioning is persistent. Proper management oversight can keep this problem in check, as can the use of scales, ladles, scoops, and spoons that can be used to dole out the correct portion sizes.
- *Watch for over cooking*. Many foods have a high moisture content, so over cooking them will result in small portion sizes – which must be supplemented

with more food. This issue can be minimized by mandating cooking times on the recipes being used.

- *Repurpose carryovers.* Any restaurant is likely to have food left over as of the close of business. If so, have a plan in place for repurposing these carryover items, so that they can still be used the next day. For example, a carryover broiled fish might be repurposed the next day as an ingredient in a seafood chowder.
- *Mandate formal drink recipes.* The pour quantity is an essential item in any drink recipe, since it places a control over the amount of alcohol poured for customers. This is a particular concern when bartenders are pouring excessively large amounts for their friends. When overpours are happening for large numbers of drinks, this can result in substantial losses.
- *Mandate the use of jiggers.* Bartenders are more likely than not to pour an excessive quantity into customer glasses. This can result in substantial losses, so mandate that they use a jigger when pouring. A jigger is a small cup used to measure alcoholic beverages. A variation on the concept is to use a metered bottle that dispenses a preset amount.
- *Train bartenders.* The bartenders should be trained and tested at regular intervals to ensure that they are able to pour standard liquor portions in drinks.
- *Implement controls to reduce employee theft.* There are many ways in which employees can steal from the business – typically either in the form of cash, food, or liquor. The controls noted later in this book can be used to reduce this theft.

Restaurant and Bar Fraud

There are several types of fraud that are unique to the operating environment of a restaurant or bar. They are as follows:

- *Voids a sale and keeps the cash.* An employee voids out a sale in the POS system after a customer has been served, and then pockets the customer's payment. A variation is to declare that a sale is complimentary after the customer has paid the bill.
- *Records a lesser sale.* An employee charges a customer the full price of a meal, but records it as a discounted senior citizen or child meal, keeping the difference.
- *Fake walkout.* An employee keeps a customer's cash payment and then claims that the customer walked out without paying.
- *Fake paid-outs.* Paid-outs are cash taken from the cash register to pay for various deliveries and miscellaneous items. Fake paid-outs end up in the pocket of the perpetrator.
- *Sells gift cards without recordation.* An employee sells restaurant gift cards, but does not ring up the sale, keeping the amount of the payment.
- *Purchases excess inventory.* An employee places orders for more inventory than the restaurant needs, and then steals the excess.

- *Kickbacks received from supplier.* A supplier pays the chef, bartender, or manager in exchange for this person funneling orders to the supplier. The supplier then overcharges the restaurant or sells it inferior-quality goods.
- *Creates a fake supplier.* The chef can create a fake supplier and send billings to the restaurant, which he or she approves for payment.
- *Does not check out.* An employee could clock in, then leaves for a while, and returns to work a later shift without having clocked out from the first shift. The result is more paid hours.
- *Drink orders not recorded.* A bartender delivers a drink to a customer, but pockets the sale amount without recording it in the POS system. This issue can be mitigated by requiring that all drink sales be recorded in the POS system before the drinks are prepared.
- *Claims that drink was returned.* A bartender can claim that a drink was returned when it was actually sold.
- *Overpouring.* A bartender may pour an excess amount of alcohol into a drink, either as a favor to friends or in an attempt to earn larger tips. This issue can be mitigated by using a jigger to measure standard liquor pours.
- *Substituted drinks.* A lower-quality liquor brand may be added to a drink, rather than the higher-cost one ordered by the customer, while charging the customer the full price and pocketing the difference.
- *Phantom bottles.* A bartender can bring in his or her own bottle of liquor and then pocket the proceeds from it, thereby denying the restaurant the margin that would otherwise have been earned on these sales.
- *Diluted drinks.* Water may be added to a drink in order to offset alcohol that has been withheld, perhaps because it was stolen. This is especially common for drinks that do not change color when water is added, such as vodka, gin, rum, or tequila.
- *Theft of alcohol.* An employee may steal alcohol, which is especially likely when there are no controls over the alcohol inventory.
- *Manual check theft.* The accountant could issue manual payroll checks to correct for supposed errors in the normal check run. The accountant then steals and cashes these checks. This can be effective in restaurant environments where there is high employee turnover, so that employees with multiple employers do not realize that extra income has been attributed to them on their Form W-2. A variation on the concept is to keep someone on the payroll for an extra pay period once they have left, and keep the payment.

Restaurant and Bar Controls

There are many controls that can be applied to a restaurant or bar. In the following subsections, we highlight some of the more critical controls pertaining to revenue, cash, inventory, payables, human resources, payroll, and risk management.

Revenue Controls

Revenue controls are concentrated around the need for a well-run POS system, proper employee training in the use of this system, and manager investigations of a variety of issues that could represent employee theft of customer payments. The controls are as follows:

- Record all guest orders in the POS system before any food or beverages are issued, so that a sale transaction is linked to each food or drink issuance.
- If manual guest checks are used, issue them to servers in a numerical sequence, so that they can be reconciled at the end of the day to see if any numbered forms are missing. For this control to work, servers must turn in all unused forms at the end of the day, and also indicate voided guest checks.
- Present guests with a bill as soon as they are finished eating, and be ready to take their payment at once. Otherwise, there is an increased risk that they will walk out without paying.
- Train employees to notify the manager at once when they see someone leaving without paying.
- Document anyone who leaves without paying, including their description, amount unpaid, and the license plate of their vehicle. This documentation should be forwarded to the police.
- Monitor all open customer orders, to ensure that all of them are eventually presented to customers for payment.
- Investigate all complimentary meals granted by the staff.
- See if coupon redemptions are unusually high with one server; this person may be using his or her own supply of coupons to charge against a guest check, and then pockets the difference.
- See if customer walkouts are concentrated with one server; this person might be claiming that customers walked out, and pocketing their payments.
- Have servers count their tip money in your presence; compare this total to their sales, to see if the tip amount is reasonable. A high tip percentage indicates that the server is providing free food or drinks to customers.

Cash Controls

Cash controls are less critical for a restaurant than used to be the case, before the prevalence of credit card and debit card payments. Consequently, we make note of a few cash controls, but not the full range of controls that used to be needed when the bulk of all customer payments were made using cash. The controls are as follows:

- Limit access to the cash register, since it is easier to oversee the work of one cashier, who is also more practiced at handling cash.
- Conduct daily cash register reconciliations.
- Investigate all cash overages and shortages, to detect instances of cashier manipulation to steal cash. In particular, look for patterns of cash overages or shortages.

- Conduct surprise cash counts.
- Never lend the cash register key to an employee, since they can copy it. Lending keys to employees should be considered a serious violation.
- Install a drop safe[5], and shift excess cash into it from the cash till. Employees should not be able to open this safe.
- Deposit all excess cash with the bank by the end of the day.
- Use a check verification service, to see if a customer has issued any bad checks. Or, use a check guarantee service, which guarantees (for a fee) that a check will be paid into the firm's checking account.
- Conduct regular bank reconciliations, and have them reviewed and approved. Someone other than the bookkeeper should conduct bank reconciliations.
- Require all cash handling personnel to take vacations each year, so that others can take over their responsibilities; this may uncover illegal activities.
- Install a video camera over the cash register.

Inventory Controls

Inventory controls are centered around the concepts of restricting purchase and withdrawal authorizations, as well as the need for a well-organized inventory system that is easy to count. The controls are as follows:

- Do not allow someone receiving inventory to also place orders for it.
- Lock all food and beverage storage areas.
- Require an authorization to remove food and beverages from inventory.
- Maintain a perpetual inventory tracking system (or at least for the most expensive items).
- Keep storage areas well-organized, making it easier to spot missing items.
- Conduct inventory counts frequently, using preprinted inventory count sheets; count high-value inventory items daily.
- Require a written request before preparing a food order.
- Record food issuances for employee meals.
- Do not allow employees to take home leftover food (since chefs might otherwise cook excess food).
- Do not allow employees to bring in knapsacks (which might be used to remove food).
- Keep the back door locked at all times, to prevent access to the inventory. Also, change the locks whenever key employees are terminated.
- Require employees to enter and exit the building through just one entrance, to see if they are removing inventory.

---

[5] A drop safe is a safe with a slot in it that allows items to be deposited without unlocking it.

Payables Controls

Payables controls are focused on avoiding excess purchases, only buying from known suppliers, and ensuring that supplier invoices are valid. The controls are as follows:

- Only accept invoices from a pre-approved list of suppliers.
- Have an authorized person approve all supplier invoices prior to payment.
- Match all supplier invoices to a receiving report before paying them.
- Verify the existence of any suppliers that you are not familiar with before paying their invoices.

Human Resources Controls

Human resources controls are not normally included in an accounting book, but we include the following controls on the grounds that many losses are caused by a firm's own staff. The controls are as follows:

- Conduct background checks on all employees.
- Require employees to take the vacation time they have earned.
- Perform exit interviews to see if anyone is willing to discuss thefts perpetrated by others.
- Take out a fidelity bond on employees. This is an insurance policy that protects against the risk that an employee will steal from the business or damage its assets. The insurer will want detailed information about each employee, so this is also a good incentive for conducting pre-employment checks on job applicants.

Payroll Controls

Payroll controls are an essential part of the system of controls for a restaurant or bar, because a large part of its expenses are derived from compensation. These controls are centered on only paying employees for the hours they have actually worked, as well as mitigating overtime costs. The controls are as follows:

- Do not allow those who verify employee hours to also prepare or sign payroll checks.
- Have the POS system deny access to those employees who have not clocked in. This ensures that they have clocked in for their shift.
- Have the payroll system deny clock ins for early arrivals and late clock outs. The intent is to ensure that the business is only paying employees for their defined shifts.
- Have the payroll system allow clock ins for different job functions, to ensure that the correct pay rate is applied to an employee. Thus, the server rate might be at quite a low pay rate (because the person is also being compensated with tips), while the host or hostess rate might be substantially higher (because the person is not receiving tips).

- Have the payroll system notify the manager when any employees are approaching 40 hours worked, so that the manager can take steps to avoid having to pay overtime.
- Create a report that lists overtime paid in descending order by employee, and then investigate those at the top of the list to see if the overtime was fraudulently claimed.

General Controls

We include several general controls that do not fall into any of the preceding controls classifications. The controls are as follows:

- Run a weekly income instatement and compare it to the results from prior weeks to look for anomalies.
- Create a weekly budget and compare actual results to it.
- Hire a third-party spotting service to watch employees for instances of theft.
- Install hidden cameras to observe the actions of employees.

Cost Markup Pricing (Meals)

A good way to establish the minimum price to be charged for food and beverages is cost markup pricing. A markup is an increase in the cost of a product to arrive at a selling price. The baseline cost upon which a markup is based is comprised of either the prime ingredients or all of the ingredients being sold. If only the cost of prime ingredients is being used, the assumption is that the costs of all other ingredients are changing in concert with the costs of the prime ingredients (which may not be the case).

The markup percentage applied to the ingredient cost is derived from an estimate of the amount of non-product costs that a restaurant or bar incurs. Examples of these costs are utilities, staff wages, and the interest expense associated with any debt.

The procedure steps to follow when formulating cost markup pricing are as follows:

1. *Compile the cost of ingredients.* It is easier to compile only the costs of prime ingredients, since there are fewer costs to track. However, this means that all remaining costs will be added to the formulation of the markup percentage, which will result in a somewhat higher markup percentage.
2. *Calculate the markup multiple.* To arrive at the markup multiple, subtract the cost of ingredients included in step 1 from all other costs of the business. It is easiest to do this using a recent income statement for the business, rather than attempting to estimate costs. Then divide the result by the total cost of ingredients to arrive at the markup percentage.
3. *Calculate prices.* Multiply the markup percentage by the cost of the ingredients to arrive at the preliminary prices to be charged.

4. *Compare to market.* Compare the resulting calculated prices to the price points being used by competitors. If the calculated prices seem unusually high or low, consider adjusting them to bring the proposed prices into closer alignment with market prices.

EXAMPLE

The manager of the Vegetarian Delight restaurant wants to use cost markup pricing to determine the price of its Tofu Tacos meal. The meal ingredients and their costs are as follows:

Ingredients	Cost
Tofu	$0.50
Tortillas	0.42
Cashews	0.08
Rice wine vinegar	0.07
Carrots	0.12
Radishes	0.10
Canola oil	0.05
Miscellaneous spices	0.03
Total cost	$1.37

Based on an analysis of the non-ingredient costs of the business, the manager determines that a 5x markup must be applied to the cost of the ingredients to derive the meal price. This calculation is:

$$\$1.37 \text{ Ingredients cost} \times 5x \text{ Markup} = \$6.85 \text{ Price}$$

An analysis of menu prices at competing restaurants reveals that a tofu tacos meal usually sells for about $6.50. After some deliberation, the manager elects to implement a price of $6.49. Doing so presents a competitive price to customers, while still approximately covering costs.

EXAMPLE

The manager of the Vegetarian Delight restaurant does not want to go to the trouble of calculating the cost of every ingredient in the Tofu Tacos meal, and so elects to base pricing on the cost of just the prime ingredients of the meal. This results in the following cost calculation:

Ingredients	Cost
Tofu	$0.50
Tortillas	0.42
Total cost	$0.92

Under this approach, more incidental ingredients are being pushed into the operating costs of the business, which means that the markup must be increased to cover these additional costs.

Based on historical experience, this means that the markup should be 7.4x. The resulting price calculation is:

$$\$0.92 \text{ Prime ingredients cost} \times 7.4x \text{ Markup} = \$6.81 \text{ Price}$$

The prime ingredient pricing approach requires less cost tracking effort by the manager, so she elects to use it as her preferred method.

There is a risk in using the prime ingredient approach. The cost basis used to derive prices may become so small and the markup percentage so large that modest changes in the cost of the prime ingredients could trigger larger changes in the calculated price. For this reason, we recommend using the cost of all ingredients when using cost markup pricing.

EXAMPLE

In the preceding example, the manager of the Vegetarian Delight restaurant elected to use the cost of just prime ingredients to derive prices, which resulted in a calculated Tofu Tacos meal price of $6.81. Subsequently, the cost of tofu increases by $0.25. When multiplied by the high 7.4x markup that the business assigns to prime ingredient costs, this means that the price of the tacos meal should be increased by $1.85. Actually enacting such a price increase would push the meal price well beyond the market rate of $6.50, probably making the meal uncompetitive.

If it is necessary to constantly adjust calculated prices by substantial amounts to bring them closer to market rates, it may be necessary to adopt a more refined technique. For example, experimentation may reveal that different markup percentages are needed for desserts or seafood. If so, cluster meals and beverages into a small number of classifications, and apply different markup percentages to each one. If this approach is used, be sure to model the outcome to make sure that the business will still generate a reasonable profit.

The Hubbart Formula

The Hubbart formula is a calculation used to derive hotel room rates; we are noting it here, because we will modify it in the next section for use in pricing meals. The Hubbart formula includes the following inputs:

- Costs incurred
- The planned profit
- The expected number of rooms that will be sold

When using the Hubbart formula, the basic process flow is as follows:

1. *Set the profit.* Determine the amount of profit that the owners of the business expect, which is based on the planned rate of return on their investment.
2. *Calculate pretax profits.* This is a simple calculation that is derived from the expected income tax rate and the profit set in the first step. The calculation is to divide the expected profit by 1 minus the expected tax rate.
3. *Determine fixed charges.* Estimate the total amount of fixed charges that will be incurred by the hotel. This includes the interest expense on any debt and management fees, as well as depreciation, property taxes, and insurance. These amounts may actually be variable – for example, there may be a floating interest rate on the debt that is based on monthly changes in the prime rate.
4. *Determine variable charges.* Estimate the total amount of variable costs that will be incurred, such as expenses for property maintenance, utilities, and operations.
5. *Determine non-room income.* Estimate the amount of income or losses generated by other services than the basic room rate. Examples are Internet access, gym access, spa activities, vending machines, and restaurant services.
6. *Calculate required room income.* This aggregate income amount is the sum of the pre-tax income, fixed charges, and variable charges derived in the preceding steps, less the net amount of non-room income.
7. *Calculate required room revenue.* This aggregate revenue amount is the sum of the required room income derived in the preceding step, plus the variable cost of the rooms (such as the payroll and payroll taxes of the room department staff). A variable cost is any cost that will not be incurred if a room is not sold.
8. *Calculate average room rate.* Divide the aggregate room revenue in the preceding step by the number of rooms that are expected to be sold.

The following example illustrates the concept.

EXAMPLE

The Cowboy Hotel is a western-themed boutique hotel located in downtown Denver. The hotel is projected to cost $12,000,000 to construct. The project is financed with a $10,000,000, 10% fixed rate loan, as well as $2,000,000 of shareholder equity. The owners would like to obtain a 15% return on their investment. The expected average income tax rate for the hotel is 21%.

Based on nearby hotels using the same operating model, the owners expect that the hotel will achieve a 70% occupancy rate. This means that the plan is to sell 25,550 rooms during the year, for which the calculation is:

$$100 \text{ Rooms} \times 70\% \text{ Occupancy rate} \times 365 \text{ Days} = 25,550 \text{ Rooms}$$

The annual fixed and variable costs of the business are as follows:

	Fixed	Variable
Administrative costs	$230,000	
Depreciation	900,000	
Insurance	40,000	
Property operations		$400,000
Property taxes	100,000	
Sales and marketing costs	130,000	
Utility costs	150,000	50,000
Totals	$1,500,000	$450,000

Additional income from departments other than rooms is summarized as follows:

Department	Income
Restaurant	$120,000
Telecommunications	20,000
Vending	10,000
Total	$150,000

The variable cost associated with each room is $15.

Based on the preceding information, the following Hubbart formula is used to derive a room rate of $142.65:

Calculation Item	Amount
1. *Set profit*: $2,000,000 investment × 15% return on investment (ROI)	$300,000
2. *Calculate pretax profits*: $300,000 ROI ÷ (1 – 21% tax rate)	$379,747
3. *Determine fixed charges*: $1,500,000 as noted in preceding table + $1,000,000 interest expense	+ 2,500,000
4. *Determine variable charges*: $450,000 as noted in preceding table	+ 450,000
5. *Determine non-room income*: $150,000 as noted in preceding table	- 150,000
6. *Calculate required room income*: Sum of items 2 through 5	$3,179,747
7. *Calculate required room revenue*:	
Add variable cost of rooms (25,550 rooms × $15 cost/room)	+ $383,250
Required room income + variable cost of rooms	$3,562,997
8. *Calculate average room rate*: $3,562,997 required room revenue ÷ 25,550 rooms	$139.45

Hubbart Formula (Meal Pricing)

The Hubbart formula can be modified and applied to the pricing of meals. The concept can be collapsed somewhat by combining fixed and variable charges with the interest expense on any debt, to create a single operating and financing expenses line item in the analysis. The primary change to the Hubbart formula is to replace the number of rooms expected to be sold (in the final step) with the expected number of meals to be served. This calculation is more difficult than the number of rooms expected to be sold, since the usual assumption is for a hotel to be open 365 days a year. A restaurant may be closed one day per week, which reduces the number of business days to 313. In addition, a restaurant may have multiple seatings per day, which increases the amount of revenue that can be generated. For example, a high-volume "fast food" restaurant may depend on a large number of seatings per day in order to generate a sufficient profit from its lower-priced menu, while a high-end restaurant that only serves dinner must rely on high prices in order to offset the effect of having just a single seating per day. The following example illustrates these concepts in an abbreviated format from what was used in the last section for the calculation of the average room rate.

EXAMPLE

French Down Home is a 40-seat restaurant that specializes in countryside French cooking, rather than haute cuisine. The owners invested $500,000 in the business and also incurred a $200,000 debt obligation at a 10% interest rate to build the restaurant. They would like to achieve a 12% return on their investment. Their incremental income tax rate is 21%. The restaurant incurs $400,000 of operating expenses per year. The historical experience with food costs is that the cost of food is 30% of revenues. By avoiding the haute cuisine label, the restaurant owners have been able to compress 3.2 seatings per day into the facility. The result appears in the following table:

Calculation Item	Amount
1. *Set profit*: $500,000 investment × 12% return on investment (ROI)	$60,000
2. *Calculate pretax profits*: $60,000 ROI ÷ (1 − 21% tax rate)	$75,949
3. *Determine operating and financing expenses*: $400,000 operating expenses + $20,000 interest expense	+ 420,000
4. *Calculate required restaurant income*: Sum of items 2 and 3	$495,949
5. *Calculate required meal revenue*: $495,949 required restaurant income ÷ meal contribution margin of 70%	$708,499
6. *Calculate average meal price*: $708,499 required restaurant revenue ÷ 40,064 meals*	$17.68

* Calculated as 313 business days × 40 seats × 3.2 seatings

There is no such thing as an average meal price in most restaurants, where customers can select from a variety of menu items. Consequently, the average price derived in the example can only be treated as a general target to be achieved.

Menu Engineering

Menu engineering is the concept of revising a restaurant menu to maximize the profitability of a restaurant. The basic underlying concept is to determine which menu items have a combination of the highest contribution margin (which is revenue minus the variable costs of a meal) and ordering popularity with customers. These items are most heavily promoted on the menu, while those meals with low contribution margins and/or low popularity are reconfigured or replaced. Menu engineering never ends, since changes in food costs will alter contribution margins over time, while meal popularity can also change.

The outcome of a menu engineering analysis can be visually presented in a variation on the product portfolio matrix popularized by the Boston Consulting Group. This matrix is comprised of four quadrants, which are labeled as follows:

- *Dogs*. Those meals having low contribution margins and low demand by customers. They should be removed from the menu whenever possible. If there is a small amount of consistent demand for them, these meals can be carried off-menu.
- *Stars*. Those meals having high contribution margins and high demand by customers. Since these meals provide a large part of a restaurant's profits, their preparation and presentation should be subject to the most exacting standards. Given their high level of popularity, customers are more likely to be insensitive to changes in price, so it makes little sense to ever discount these menu items. If anything, the reverse is the case – customers are more likely to accept price increases on these items.
- *Question marks*. Those meals having high contribution margins but low demand by customers. Given the high margin, it can be worthwhile to attempt a repackaging of these meals, or perhaps different placement on the menu. The low popularity level may be caused by an excessively high price, so consider experimenting with modest price reductions to see if this sparks an increase in demand.
- *Workhorses*. Those meals having low contribution margins and high demand by customers. These meals may be considered by customers to be the foundation of a restaurant's offerings. If so, make changes only with the greatest care; this could include minor price increases over a long period of time, or a slight placement change to a less-obvious part of the menu.

The derivation of a product portfolio matrix is described in the following example.

EXAMPLE

The owners of the All American Grill decide to conduct a menu engineering analysis of 12 items on the restaurant's menu, based on information obtained during the past month. This results in the following table that presents the contribution margin and customer order volume for each item:

Menu Item	Contribution Margin	Number Ordered
Pork chops	$10.15	260
Baby back ribs	9.00	235
Porterhouse	12.80	190
Grilled chicken	3.75	375
Ribeye steak	7.75	30
Sirloin	6.25	500
Salmon	3.50	90
Halibut	8.50	65
Crab cakes	8.10	55
Lobster	14.70	100
Enchiladas	4.25	70
Burrito	4.00	600

These results are then placed on the following product portfolio matrix, where it is apparent that the worst meals are the salmon, crab cakes, and enchiladas, which generate neither volume nor a notable contribution margin.

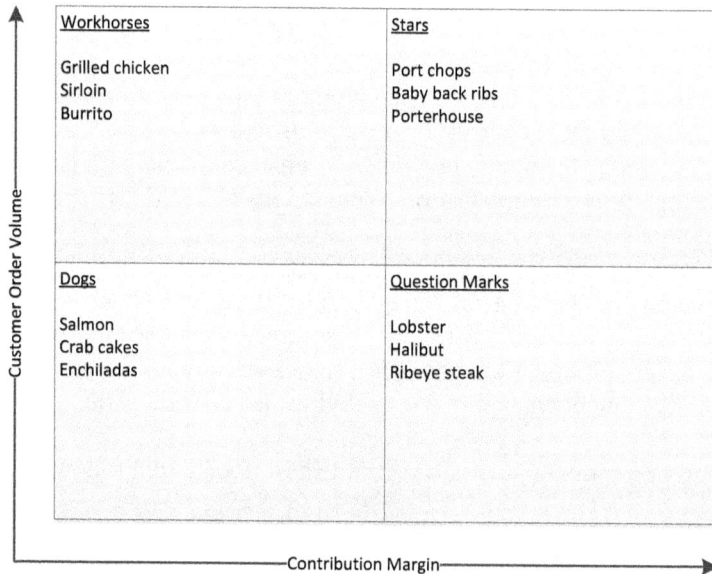

Workhorses Grilled chicken Sirloin Burrito	**Stars** Port chops Baby back ribs Porterhouse
Dogs Salmon Crab cakes Enchiladas	**Question Marks** Lobster Halibut Ribeye steak

Customer Order Volume ↑ — Contribution Margin →

Another analysis tool for your menu is the *popularity index*, which indicates which menu items are popular with guests. It is calculated as the total number of a specific menu item that were sold in the measurement period, divided by the total number of all menu items sold. While this measurement will provide you with an easy analysis of what is most popular with customers, it will not indicate which of these items is the most profitable – so use it with caution.

Restaurant and Bar Operating Ratios

Ratio analysis is a useful way to review the operations and financial results of a restaurant or bar. Managers are most concerned with the utilization of their facility and the revenue generated from each customer. Additional measurements track the costs of food, beverages, and labor. These analyses are expanded upon within this section.

Average Food Service Check

The average food service check is the total revenue from food sales divided by the number of customers served. The intent of this measurement is to determine the average amount that each person pays for a meal. When combined with the seat turnover figure described in the following sub-section, you can obtain a reasonable picture of the drivers that generate restaurant and bar revenue.

EXAMPLE

The owner of the Crumb Cake Café has recently instituted a menu change in which prices were increased on a selection of meals. He wants to determine the impact on the average food service check and so compiles the following calculation for the month immediately before and after the menu change:

	Month Before Menu Change	Month After Menu Change
Total food revenue	$29,136	$30,505
Total customers served	4,800	4,620
Average food service check	$6.07	$6.60

The table reveals that the average food service check has indeed risen but also that the total number of customers served has declined. This could mean that some customers are reacting to the price increase by going elsewhere. It could be useful to track the trend of total customers served on a trend line, to see if the decline persists.

This calculation can be broken down into several smaller areas in order to gain a more granular knowledge of revenues. For example, the calculation could be broken out just for beverage sales, or separately for the breakfast, lunch, and dinner periods, or separately for take-out food versus the main dining area.

Seat Turnover

Seat turnover is the number of people served, divided by the number of seats available for use. A high seat turnover level is of particular importance when menu items sell at lower price points, since a restaurant has to generate a profit by serving the largest possible number of customers.

The seat turnover measurement is usually subdivided into meal periods, so there is one turnover measurement for breakfast, another for lunch, and another for dinner.

EXAMPLE

The Harvest Restaurant has 110 seats available for use, and offers lunch and dinner. On the preceding day, Harvest served 284 customers during lunch and 204 during dinner. This resulted in the following seat turnover ratios:

	Lunch	Dinner
Number of customers served	284	204
Seats available	110	110
Seat turnover	2.6x	1.9x

Though the restaurant clearly serves a larger volume of customers at lunch, the average price per meal served is less expensive during that meal, so the greater seat turnover is needed in order to generate an adequate profit.

The seat turnover measurement can be misleading. It is possible that a person served will not have actually purchased an entire meal, but rather just a coffee or a dessert, and so generates less revenue. Also, the seating configuration can reduce the calculated amount of seat turnover. For example, if all of the available seating is for tables of four, a party of two will take up two extra seats for the duration of their meal.

Sales Mix

Sales mix refers to the proportions of different products and services that comprise the total sales of a restaurant or bar. In most cases, each product or service provided has a different contribution margin, so changes in sales mix (even if the total sales level remains the same) usually result in differing amounts of profit.

EXAMPLE

The accountant of Creekside Pizza is examining the sales and profit figures for the past two quarters, and is having difficulty understanding why sales were identical, but profits were radically different in the two periods. He creates the following analysis of sales of the company's two types of pizza:

	First Quarter			Second Quarter		
	Pizza A	Pizza B	Total	Pizza A	Pizza B	Total
Sales	$200,000	$350,000	$550,000	$400,000	$150,000	$550,000
Variable costs	160,000	140,000	300,000	320,000	60,000	380,000
Variable cost %	80%	40%	55%	80%	40%	69%
Contribution	40,000	210,000	250,000	80,000	90,000	170,000
Fixed costs			200,000			200,000
Profit (loss)			$50,000			-$30,000

Because sales have shifted between the two products, which have radically different contribution margins, the profit level is heavily impacted by the sales mix.

Ratio of Beverage to Food Revenue

This is total beverage revenue divided by food revenue. The reason for using this measurement is to spot any declines in the proportion of beverage revenue. This can be of some importance, since beverage sales are usually highly profitable. A decline can be counteracted with a marketing campaign and menu revisions that focus on more beverage sales.

EXAMPLE

Arturo's Sports Bar is normally quite profitable, primarily due to the hard-drinking sports crowd that watches a variety of sports on the big-screen televisions prominently displayed throughout the facility. In recent months, following a dining room reconstruction project, profitability has dipped. To determine why, the manager calculates the ratio of beverage to food revenue for a typical week before and after a recent overhaul of the dining area. The results are as follows:

	Week Before Overhaul	Week After Overhaul
Total beverage revenue	$11,200	$9,500
Total food revenue	$39,200	$49,500
Beverage to food ratio	28.6%	19.2%

The culprit turns out to have been the dining room overhaul. Customers are so comfortable in the new dining area that they no longer gravitate to the bar area, and so spend more on food and less on beverages.

Food Cost Percentage

The food cost percentage is a comparison of the total cost of food sold to food sales. A restaurant manager may find it necessary to increase prices as food costs increase, depending on the level of local competition. An increased food cost percentage may also be due to poor portion control, theft, waste, or spoilage. This is one of the largest restaurant costs, and so should be closely followed on a trend line to more easily spot variances from the long-term cost percentage.

EXAMPLE

The owner of the Spaghetti Western restaurant has been tracking the food cost percentage of his restaurant for several years, and has recently noticed a five percent spike in food costs. The types of food purchased have not changed during that time, nor have the food suppliers. However, there *have* been some changes in the kitchen staff. Upon closer investigation, he realizes that the new employees are plating meals with slightly larger portion sizes, which accounts for the increase in the food cost percentage. He institutes additional training to standardize portion sizes.

Beverage Cost Percentage

The beverage cost percentage is a comparison of the total cost of beverages sold to beverage sales. It can be refined further, to examine the beverage cost by type of beverage sold. There are many issues that can cause beverage costs to rise. Consider the following issues that just relate to the sale of beer:

- *Free beer*. Free beer can be considered a marketing avenue to building brand loyalty, but it may just keep customers coming back for more free beer.
- *Overpours*. Pouring too much results in outgoing beer for which there is no corresponding cash inflow.
- *Inventory turnover*. Once a keg has been tapped, it will go bad in about five days.
- *Foam waste*. The presence of too much foam represents lost beer, since about 25 percent of foam is beer.

EXAMPLE

The Slobbering Dog Bar has experienced a sharp increase in its beer cost percentage, costing the bar $4,000 in lost profits during the most recent month. Further investigation reveals that its kegs have been getting too warm. When this happens, excess carbon dioxide is released, causing foam to erupt. To avoid this, the bar manager instructs her staff to store the beer at 38 degrees Fahrenheit. To prevent foaming once beer leaves the keg, she also ensures that the lines are maintained at the same 38-degree temperature.

Labor Cost Percentage

The labor cost percentage is a comparison of all compensation, payroll taxes, and fringe benefits to total restaurant sales. It can be refined further, to examine the labor cost of specific areas within a restaurant. This is a major cost, and so needs to be tightly controlled.

EXAMPLE

The Pesky Brew Pub has traditionally closed at 8 p.m., due to a city ordinance that does not allow beer sales after that time. However, the ordinance has recently been changed to extend beer sales to 11 p.m. The owner of Pesky is cautious about opening for the extra hours, since he will need to pay at least four staff during these extra hours, and it is uncertain how many patrons will continue to pay for beers between 8 p.m. and 11 p.m. After running the pub during these extended hours for a month, the owner concludes that the incremental revenues are not enough to pay for the incremental labor costs past a 9 p.m. closing time; after that time, sales drop off too much to make it worthwhile to keep the pub open.

Contribution by Meal Period

Breakfast meals tend to be less expensive than lunches, which in turn are less expensive than dinners. This also holds true for the contribution margin associated with each type of meal – the margin per meal is least for breakfast, better for lunch and best for dinner. A restaurant can improve the profitability situation for these earlier meals by increasing the number of seatings. For example, a dinner that has a contribution margin of $50 but only one seating generates the same total contribution margin as a lunch that has a contribution margin of $10 and five seatings.

While the interrelationship of contribution margin and the number of seatings is simple enough, it can be a significant financial problem for a restaurant manager who does not keep track of trends in these numbers, as noted in the following example.

EXAMPLE

The Family Empanadas restaurant serves hearty Argentine fare to its customers during lunch and dinner. During the past year, the business experienced the following results for its lunches and dinners:

	Number of Seats		Number of Seatings		Number of Days		Contribution per Meal		Total Contribution
Lunch	60	×	2.1	×	313	×	$5.75	=	$226,769
Dinner	60	×	1.5	×	313	×	10.70	=	301,419
Total									$528,188

A new generation of the family takes over the restaurant, and promptly invests in a makeover that is designed to make the restaurant more comfortable, including gas log fireplaces and more plush booths. The intent was to provide a better experience for which customers would be more likely to pay higher prices. The price increase worked, with solid increases in the contribution per meal. However, the environment has become so inviting that no one wants to leave, resulting in much lower seatings for both lunch and dinner. The result appears in the following table, where the restaurant's total contribution has declined by $31,833.

	Number of Seats		Number of Seatings		Number of Days		Contribution per Meal		Total Contribution
Lunch	60	×	1.7	×	313	×	$6.90	=	$220,289
Dinner	60	×	1.2	×	313	×	12.25	=	276,066
Total									$496,355

In essence, lack of attention to the factors causing the number of seatings to change has resulted in a reduction in the total contribution margin of the restaurant.

Additional Restaurant and Bar Ratios

Here are several additional ratios that might be of interest, depending on the circumstances:

- Sales per square foot
- Sales per employee
- Food inventory turnover
- Liquor inventory turnover
- Occupancy costs per square foot
- Profit as a percentage of sales
- Profit per seat

Summary

Restaurants and bars can generate remarkably low profit margins, so it makes sense to have a robust accounting system in place that contains strong controls, while also reporting on revenue and cost trends in sufficient detail for managers to take action on any unfavorable variances. Underpinning such a system is a deep knowledge of how employee fraud can occur, the controls needed to stop it, and the accounting processes required to generate accurate financial reports in a timely manner.

Glossary

A

Accumulated depreciation. The total depreciation for a fixed asset that has been charged to expense since that asset was acquired and made available for use.

Adjusting entry. A journal entry used at the end of an accounting period to adjust the balances in various general ledger accounts to more closely align the reported results and financial position of a business to meet the requirements of an accounting framework.

B

Bank balance. The ending cash balance appearing on the bank statement for a bank account.

C

Capitalization limit. The amount paid for an asset, above which it is recorded as a long-term asset. If the amount paid is less than the capitalization limit, then the amount paid is instead charged to expense in the period incurred.

Chart of accounts. A listing of all accounts used in a restaurant's general ledger.

D

Depreciation. The charging to expense of a portion of an asset that relates to the revenue generated by that asset.

Direct operating expenses. The aggregation of a number of smaller expenses related to the running of a restaurant.

Drop safe. A safe with a slot in it that allows items to be deposited without unlocking it.

F

Finance lease. When a contract permits the use of an asset, and transfers ownership to the lessee after the lease period is complete.

First in, first out. An accounting concept which assumes that the first units received are the first ones used.

G

Guest check. A detailed listing of all the menu items ordered by a customer.

H

House account. When a restaurant or bar allows a customer to put purchases on a tab and later pay in a lump sum, after multiple visits.

J

Jigger. A bar tool for measuring and pouring alcohol.

M

MACRS. The Modified Accelerated Cost Recovery System, which states the periodic depreciation rate that can be applied to fixed assets.

Menu engineering. The examination of the contribution margins of and demand for meal items, which is used to configure a menu to direct customers toward those meals that will generate the highest net profit for a restaurant.

O

Operating lease. When the lessee has obtained the use of an underlying asset for only a period of time.

P

Par level. The minimum amount of inventory needed to meet customer demand, while providing a cushion in case of any unexpected demand.

Popularity index. A measurement that indicates which menu items are popular with guests.

Profit center. A business unit within a restaurant that generates revenues and profits or losses.

R

Reversing entry. A journal entry made in an accounting period that reverses selected entries made in the immediately preceding period.

S

Sales tax. A tax imposed on the sale of tangible personal property and certain services, and is calculated as a percentage of the sales price.

Salvage value. A presumed value of a fixed asset at the end of its useful life.

T

Tip credit. When an employer credits a portion of an employee's tips toward the employer's obligation to pay the employee the minimum wage.

U

Unit of measure. The standard unit of measurement used when accounting for stock.

Useful life. The time period over which it is expected that an asset will be productive.

W

Walkout. A customer who leaves a restaurant without paying.

Index

www.ingramcontent.com/pod-product-compliance
Lightning Source LLC
Chambersburg PA
CBHW051417200326
41520CB00023B/7268